IRISH RUGBY
TOP 50 PLAYERS

FOREWORD BY OLLIE CAMPBELL

IRISH RUGBY
TOP 50 PLAYERS

First published in the UK in 2015

© G2 Entertainment Ltd 2020

www.G2ent.co.uk

Printed and bound printed in Europe

ISBN 978-1-782818-44-1

Contents

04 Foreword

06 Introduction

27 Best

30 Bowe

32 Campbell

34 Crawford

36 Clohessy

38 D'Arcy

40 Davidson

42 Dawson

44 Dempsey

46 Duggan

48 Earls

50 Easterby

52 Elwood

54 Foley

56 Furlong

58 Geoghegan

60 Gibson

62 Hayes

65 Healy

67 Heaslip

70 Hickie

72 Horgan

74 Humphreys

76 Keane

78 Kearney

81 Kiernan

82 Kyle

84 McBride

86 McKay

89 Millar

91 Miller

93 Mullen

94 Mulcahy

96 Murphy

98 Murray

100 O'Brien

102 O'Callaghan

104 O'Connell

106 O'Driscoll

110 O'Gara

112 O'Kelly

114 O'Mahony

116 O'Reilly

118 Sexton

120 Slattery

122 Stockdale

124 Stringer

126 Trimble

128 Wallace

130 Wood

Foreword

Ireland's first ever rugby international was against England at Kennington Oval in London on Feb 15th 1875, when rugby was a 20 a side game. Since that auspicious day various Irish teams have produced many unforgettable memories, many exceptional players and more than its fair share of exceptional characters too. During "The Troubles" on this island in the '70s the lovable and unique Moss Keane once memorably said that "there are no borders in an Irish dressing room". It is with this inclusive sentiment in mind that I am privileged to introduce this enthralling book on behalf of every player who has ever pulled on the famous green jersey of Ireland.

One of those players was the immortal Cameron Michael Henderson [Mike] Gibson one of my childhood heroes who I idolised and was fortunate to play with. He once wrote that "rugby is like love; it is a game of touch and of feel and of instinct". It seems to me that Liam McCann and Jules Gammond have written this book with the same love of the game as those they have written about played it.

It's been said that books are the quietest and most constant of friends and I am sure this book will be a quiet and constant friend to anyone who reads it for years to come and it will be a welcome and worthy addition to the ever-growing anthology on Irish rugby and its players.

Ollie Campbell,
Ireland & British and Irish Lions flyhalf

Introduction

Primitive forms of rugby had been played for hundreds of years (notably in Ireland where the 1527 Statute of Galway allowed football but banned an early form of hurling called hokie), although the innovation of being allowed to run with the ball was certainly a turning point. William Webb Ellis's father was stationed in Ireland with the Dragoons so he would have noticed locals playing the game of *Caid* (meaning scrotum of the bull) in either its field (the ball must pass between two marked trees) or cross-country (the ball must cross a parish boundary) forms. The Welsh believe field *Caid* derived from their Criapan, which the Cornish called *Hurling* to *Goales,* and dated from the Bronze Age.

Whether Webb Ellis picked up the ball and ran in 1823 is unclear but the game certainly changed at Rugby School around this time. It also must have become more popular outside school because the kicking and running forms were outlawed by the Highways Act of 1835, which forbade their playing on public land by the common man. Instead, the sport found refuge in other public schools, although why the rules laid down at Rugby have survived, while those at Cheltenham, Shrewsbury and Marlborough haven't is unclear, but it seems likely that Rugby's influential headmaster, Dr Thomas Arnold, lobbied for their laws to be universally applied. By the mid-1860s many schools abided by the Rugby rules.

As pupils left school and went to university, they took the game with them. Old Rugbeians challenged Old Etonians to a game of football at Cambridge University in 1839, with the Rugbeians using their hands to secure victory. As a result, representatives of the major public schools met to draw up the Cambridge rules of 1848. In 1863, another meeting outlawed hacking and tripping. Then, in 1871, three Old Rugbeians and Edwin Ash of Richmond called a meeting of 21 clubs – to be chaired by Richmond captain E.C. Holmes – at the Pall Mall restaurant in Regent Street, and together they formed the Rugby Football Union. Trinity College and Blackrock College in Dublin immediately became rugby strongholds.

The 1870s saw the game spread around the world, first to Australia and New Zealand and then to Canada and the United States. In 1875, British troops stationed in Cape Town introduced the game to South Africa. It was during this period that the formations changed markedly. Numbers were reduced to 15-a-side, usually 10 forwards and five backs, although there were variations. As the game changed in Eng-

land, it also spawned gridiron in the USA, with the scrum being replaced with the line of scrimmage and forward passes being allowed. In Ireland, football and rugby merged to form Gaelic Football, a 15-man game involving kicking and running with the ball in hand. Played predominantly in Melbourne, rugby

also evolved to produce Australian Rules.

The field game of Gaelic Football pre-dates rugby by some time but it wasn't until 1884 that the Gaelic Athletic Association (GAA) was formed, and it wasn't until 1887 that the game was codified. There are now around 2,500 clubs in Ireland, the best 32 of which annually contest the Sam Maguire Trophy for the right to be called All-Ireland champions. The ball may not be thrown in either the Gaelic or Australian variants, rather it must be struck with the hand. In Gaelic Football the ball can be passed in any direction to score a goal in a net under the rugby-style H posts, or a point if it crosses above the bar.

The Irish Rugby Football Union was founded in 1874 and the first England-Ireland match took place the following year. Shortly afterwards, the number of players was reduced from 20-a-side to 15. They were usually arranged with 10 forwards, two attacking half-backs and three defensive backs, but some teams swapped a defensive back for an attacking half-back who became the first three-quarter. Cardiff then developed a short passing move to the flying half-back, which was later shortened to fly-half. In 1877, England beat Ireland by two goals and two tries to nil in the first 15-a-side international.

With the first matches being played between the home nations from 1871 onwards, it was only a matter of time before a championship was devised, although it took another decade before Ireland won their first match. The first championship was played in 1883, with England winning. The tournament that developed from these early encounters was originally called the Home Nations Championship when contested by England, Ireland, Scotland and Wales. When France joined in 1910, it became the Five Nations, and finally the Six Nations when Italy joined in 2000.

In 1884, Ireland arrived in Cardiff to play Wales with only 13 men. The Welsh generously lent them two players but the Irish still lost. It would take another three years before they won their first match at Lansdowne Road, a long-awaited win over England by two goals to nil. In 1888, the side finally registered a win over a Wales team that was about to enter its first golden era.

In 1891, the Irish fullback Dolway Walkington caught a loose kick against the Welsh at Stradey Park, Llanelli. Then, as he was very short-sighted, he calmly removed his monocle and dropped a perfect goal. It was reported that he would remove the eyepiece before every tackle, and that he'd taken it out for a crucial conversion against England in Dublin in 1880, which he then missed.

The Irish eventually adopted the Welsh system of eight forwards and seven backs, and in 1894 they recorded back-to-back wins over England and Scotland. Vic-

LEFT A portrait of Dr Thomas Arnold by Thomas Phillips

BELOW The 1928 original Sam Maguire Cup in the GAA museum

tory over Wales in Belfast gave the Irish their first Triple Crown. Rugby was still a game for the protestant middle class, however. Only the great Tom Crean bridged the religious divide, but political differences were often put aside when the Irish took the field and they claimed two more championships (1896 and 1899) before the end of the century.

Scotland and Wales had dominated the tournament thus far and they had contributed the most players to the first touring sides to the leave the UK over the previous two decades. The 1891 tour, for example, was more about establish-

ing rugby as a sport in South Africa, and, despite the drubbing dished out by the tourists – South African sides only scored one point throughout the entire tour – the British team saw interest in the sport surge. The tourists also presented the Currie Cup to Griqualand West. This is still South African rugby's biggest domestic prize.

This was the last time for nearly a century that any British side had things so easy in South Africa. Although the tourists won the 1896 series, the hosts had learned their lesson and only went down narrowly. This tour saw more players from Ireland joining the party. They were becoming a major force in the Home Nations Championship and had just won a Triple Crown. The pack was built around the inspiring number eight, Tommy Crean, and Fred Byrne's record of 100 points on the tour lasted until 1960. Alf Larard made South African rugby history by scoring his country's first international try in the final Test at Newlands.

Sides from the southern hemisphere soon realised they could make an impact if they toured the British Isles, with any victories greatly enhancing personal reputations and that of the sport back home. In 1905, the All Blacks visited Dublin for

BELOW The first Irish rugby team in 1875

a match against Ireland that became the first all-ticket international in rugby history. The Irish modified their line-up, shunning the traditional Welsh formation and copying the visitors by swapping one forward for a back. The gamble failed and the Kiwis romped home 15-0. South Africa visited in 1906 and they also beat the Irish in Belfast, although the 15-12 score flattered the tourists.

Southern hemisphere rugby continued stealing the north's thunder on the next overseas trip by the British Isles, despite the tourists boasting a core of exceptional Welsh backs like William Llewellyn, Percy Bush, Rhys Gabe, Tommy Vile and Edward Morgan, as well as promising young Irishmen like Charlie Patterson and Reg

SÓUTH AFRICAN TEAM v. GREAT BRITAIN AT KIMBERLEY, 1891
SUID-AFRIKAANSE SPAN t. BRITTANJE IN KIMBERLEY, 1891

LEFT The South African team that faced the British Isles in 1891

Back/Agter: Arthur Solomon; A. de Kock (G.W.); J. T. Vigne (T.); J. Louw (T.); B. H. Heatlie (W.P.); D. Smith (G.W.); A. Richards (W.P.); C. Versfeld.

Middle/Middel: E. Alexander (G.W.); R. Shand (G.W.); R. C. Sneddon (captain/kaptein, G.W.); M. Versfeld (W.P.); B. Duff (W.P.).

Front/Voor: W. Trenery (G.W.); J. M. Powell (G.W.); C. W. Smith (G.W.); H. C. Boyes (G.W.).

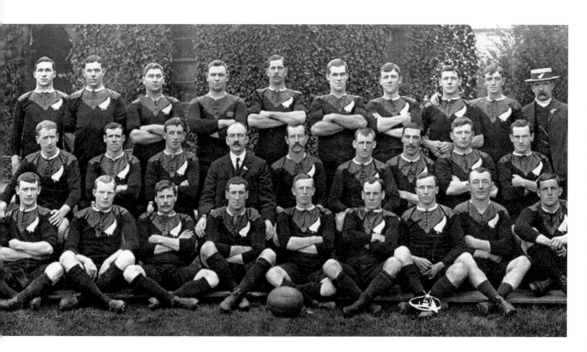

RIGHT James
Frederick Byrne

time in 1909. They ran in a record five tries and won 19-8. The following year, Ireland was well represented on the British Lions tour to South Africa. It was the first trip that officially represented the four home unions, but the Lions couldn't contain the Springboks and lost two of the three Tests. A second touring party visited Argentina and enjoyed greater success.

Edwards. Bush came to international recognition and was the difference on the Australian leg, although the All Blacks were a different proposition and used the soon-to-be-outlawed 2-3-2 formation in the pack. The 1908 trip saw a change in strip because the Scottish and Irish unions weren't represented. The Anglo-Welsh squad wore red jerseys with a thick white band reflecting the combination of the countries, but they struggled in Australia and could only manage nine wins from 17 games. They were also hammered in two of the three Tests in New Zealand.

Ireland played France for the first

South Africa toured Ireland again in 1912 and this time they gave the hosts no chance, running in 10 unanswered tries and winning by a record margin that still stands: 38-0. As Ireland had shared the Five Nations Championship with England earlier in the year, this heavy defeat dented morale and Irish rugby entered a lean period that brought little success until the mid-1920s.

Ireland kicked off the 1926 Five Nations campaign with a resounding 11-0 win over France and they then scraped past England in Dublin by just four points. A 3-0 win over Scotland left them only needing victory over Wales to secure a first Grand Slam. The dream died in Swansea, however, as the Welsh squeezed home by three points. For the next two years it was the English who denied the Irish a Grand Slam and the side slumped to mid-table by 1929.

With the French having been expelled from the tournament for apparently paying players (thereby breaking the rules on amateurism), England, Ireland and Wales shared the title with two wins apiece in 1932. Ireland only won a single match in 1933 and 1934 but topped the championship table with wins over Scotland and Wales in 1935. A one-point loss to eventual champions England denied the Irish a clean sweep in 1937 but they shared the last championship before the war.

The French were readmitted to the Five Nations in 1947 but it would take until the following year before Ireland finally broke their duck and recorded a Grand Slam. Their first match was a comfortable win over France in Paris on New Year's Day but the big test came six weeks later at Twickenham. Karl Mullen, a 21-year-old medical student, was appointed captain before the game. He was a great tactician but also instilled

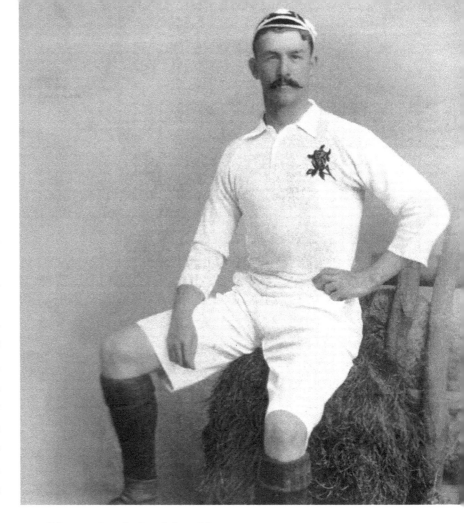

confidence that helped the side overcome their pre-game nerves. He said afterwards that he had a feeling they couldn't lose if everyone played their best.

His conviction was no doubt strengthened by the man playing at fly-half. Jack Kyle has repeatedly been voted Ireland's greatest player by the Irish Rugby Football Union and it was rare for the opposition to lay a hand on him. Team-mate Jim McCarthy once joked that he often

BELOW Wales take on Ireland at Cardiff Arms Park in 1932

didn't need to have his shorts cleaned after games because he'd not been tackled once.

McCarthy joined Des O'Brien and Bill McKay in a formidable back row that earned the nickname 'Kyle's Outriders' because of the level of protection they gave the genius at number 10. The fly-half wasn't without his faults, however, and a rush of blood almost cost Ireland the Grand Slam: the visitors were leading

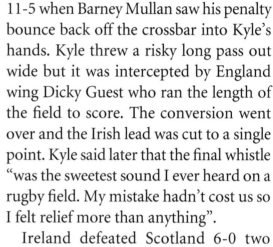

11-5 when Barney Mullan saw his penalty bounce back off the crossbar into Kyle's hands. Kyle threw a risky long pass out wide but it was intercepted by England wing Dicky Guest who ran the length of the field to score. The conversion went over and the Irish lead was cut to a single point. Kyle said later that the final whistle "was the sweetest sound I ever heard on a rugby field. My mistake hadn't cost us so I felt relief more than anything".

Ireland defeated Scotland 6-0 two weeks later so the championship would be decided against Wales at Ravenhill in Belfast. It was extremely difficult to cross the border after the war but 30,000 fans arrived hoping to see the men in green make history. The players only found out if they'd been selected by listening to Radio Athlone on the Sunday before and they then had a single half-hour training session on the Friday to prepare for the biggest game of their careers.

Mullen knew that Welsh scrum-half Haydn Tanner posed the greatest threat to his side so he instructed O'Brien to tackle him out of the game. The Welsh had prepared for a physical confrontation too, however, and they brought plenty of menace. They also had Bleddyn Williams, one of the game's greatest

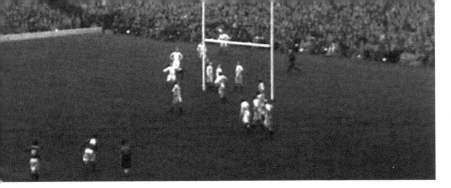

existed, the Five Nations was the only international tournament for Europe's top players and winning a Grand Slam elevated you from mere mortal to sporting deity. Mullen remembered the elation and sense of achievement lasting for several weeks, and people asked him for the next

LEFT The Irish kick a goal

BELOW The victorious team leave the field

centres, and it was he who almost ruined the party with a breathtaking solo score. The Welsh forwards continually tried to rough Mullen up but he kept his cool and delivered a crucial pass to O'Brien, who then kicked beyond the Welsh defence. Prop John Daly drifted through the red jerseys to touch down for the vital score and a nation was released from its torment.

Daly was carried from the pitch by ecstatic fans who ripped the shirt off his back and tore it to pieces to sell in the pubs after the match. He too had an eventful night as he was arrested after a run-in with several Orangemen and spent a night in the cells. He then vanished on the way back to Dublin and turned up with rugby league side Huddersfield after losing his job.

Before the World Cup

ABOVE Michael Kiernan releases the backs during the 1982 Triple Crown

they won the Test series easily. They returned home to play their last match at Ravenhill in Belfast as, from 1955 until 2007, the troubles in the province prevented them from playing in Northern Ireland.

The following decade marked a low point in Irish rugby, although several disappointing Five Nations campaigns were punctuated with glorious one-off performances, such as when they beat South Africa for the first time in 1965 and Australia in 1967. Later in the year, they became the first of the home nations to beat a southern hemisphere team away when they turned the Wallabies over in Sydney.

By the end of the decade, Irish fortunes were reviving, although the glorious Welsh team of the same era denied them a Grand Slam in 1969. Both Wales and Ireland were unbeaten when the 1972 championship was abandoned in the face of threats from the IRA. All the sides won two matches in 1973, and the Irish would have registered their first win over the All Blacks later in the year had they not missed a last-minute conversion.

The 23-year wait for an outright championship finally came to an end

60 years what it was like to be the architect of the historic 1948 Grand Slam.

Much of the same team secured a Triple Crown in the 1949 championship, but a draw against Wales in Cardiff in the last match of the 1951 season prevented another Triple Crown and Grand Slam. The side toured Argentina in 1952 and

when Ireland won the 1974 Five Nations by virtue of a 9-9 draw with Wales. The 1970s were dominated by the Welsh, however, and it took until 1982 before Ireland had another shot at a Grand Slam. They saw off Wales 20-12 in Dublin and overcame England by a point at Twickenham. Scotland were also beaten in the Triple Crown match but the Irish weren't strong enough to beat the French in Paris.

Having spent so long in the international wilderness, Ireland surprised their critics with another Triple Crown in 1985 but a 15-15 draw with the French in Dublin scuppered their chances of a second Grand Slam.

With the Welsh still in decline, the French dominated the Five Nations for the remainder of the decade. Australia and New Zealand, meanwhile, began to make noises about a possible World Cup. They had already submitted separate bids, which had been turned down by the IRB, so they joined forces and resubmitted a more comprehensive bid to co-host the first tournament. They suggested staging it in 1987 so it didn't clash with the Olympic Games or the FIFA World Cup and presented their feasibility study to the IRB in 1985. When France threw

their weight behind a tournament in the southern hemisphere (on the condition that countries not affiliated to the IRB would also be invited), the IRB was forced into a corner and had to take a vote. South Africa voted in favour, even though they would be excluded from any tournament due to apartheid, and this prompted England and Wales to follow suit. Only Ireland and Scotland voted against the tournament as they felt it threatened the game's amateur status. The IRB went with the vote and New Zealand and Australia hosted the event in 1987.

Ireland lost to Wales in their group but victories over Canada and Tonga saw them qualify for a quarter-final against Australia in Sydney. The hosts were too powerful in every department and ran out 33-15 winners, but matches between the two at subsequent World Cups became the stuff of sporting legend.

Ireland had seen off Zimbabwe and Japan in the pool stage of the 1991 World Cup but they were under par in their final group match against Scotland. Second place in the group meant a quarter-final berth against an Australian team that had easily overcome Argentina, Western Samoa and Wales.

Ireland had home advantage at Lans-

ABOVE David Campese clears the danger as the Irish close in

ese were all held up just short of the Irish line but Campese then took a crash ball in midfield and burst through the cover defence to score his 44th international try.

When Ralph Keyes slotted a difficult penalty off the post, Ireland tried to up the tempo but ferocious Australian defence pegged them deep within their own half. Keyes managed to kick another penalty to bring Ireland level eight minutes before the break, however.

Lynagh took advantage of more Irish indiscipline early in the second half and restored a three-point lead for the Wallabies, but Keyes countered with a snap drop-goal. When Australia unleashed their backs for the first time in the half, Marty Roebuck and Jason Little combined in midfield to allow Campese to score in the corner after. Lynagh added the extra points and Australia led by six. Campese made two try-saving tackles to deny a potent Irish backline that included Brendan Mullin and Simon Geoghegan, but Keyes scored another penalty after Australia slowed the ball down illegally.

The Australian backs then tried the same midfield move that had worked twice before and the Irish fell for it again. Referee Jim Fleming disallowed the try, however, deeming that Jason Little hadn't released

downe Road and they showed their intent early with an expansive game. Indiscipline at the breakdown gave Michael Lynagh an early shot at goal, but, although he missed, Australia maintained the pressure. Lynagh, Horan and Camp-the ball when half-tackled by Geoghegan in the build-up. Campese broke through the Irish defence again shortly afterwards but his deft chip went dead.

The Irish then broke up-field from a scrum in their own half. Jim Staples kicked through for Jack Clarke to chase and he beat Campese to the ball. He popped it inside to flanker Gordon Hamilton and the big back-row forward galloped home from 40 metres. Lansdowne Road erupted as the Irish took a one-point lead with five minutes to play. Keyes kicked the conversion and it seemed as if the Australians would be dumped out of the tournament.

The Wallabies didn't panic, however. They used the same midfield move to get position in the Irish 22, and used a similar set play to free Campese on the right-hand side. He couldn't evade Staples's cover tackle but the ball popped up to Lynagh and the fly-half scored in the corner to break Irish hearts.

The 1995 and 1999 tournaments were both disappointing for the men in green. In South Africa they were knocked out by France in the quarter-final, and in Wales they were forced through the playoffs to reach the quarter-final. They suffered an embarrassing loss to Argentina, however, and were eliminated. They'd performed poorly in the Five Nations since 1985 and the bigger stage was proving equally uncompromising.

The side underperformed in the first three years of the Six Nations, and they then lost a Grand Slam decider against future World Champions England in 2003. The World Cup later that year finally gave the side the chance to avenge the defeat to Australia as the two teams met in the group stage of the tournament. It turned into another classic that would decide who topped the pool.

Australia started quickly and spent the first 15 minutes camped in the Irish 22 but they only came away with a George Gregan drop goal. They continued applying pressure and Wendell Sailor almost breached the Irish line twice. Stephen Larkham realised the Irish were short of numbers out wide, however, so he released Joe Roff with a huge cross-field pass. George Smith took the final ball and scored in the corner moments later.

Ronan O'Gara pulled three points back with a penalty after quarter of an hour but Elton Flatley restored Australia's eight-point lead with a 40-metre kick. Irish hooker Keith Wood then inspired a brief fight-back but Ireland couldn't

ABOVE Ireland briefly
relocated to Croke Park
while Lansdowne Road
was being redeveloped

alty after pulling George Smith down by the hair. Flatley missed the kick but Ireland gave away another two minutes later and this time he knocked it over. O'Gara missed a difficult kick but Ireland almost forced a try after a prolonged period of pressure. The Irish turned down two penalties from the resulting scrum and, having chosen to run rather than kick, O'Driscoll beat Sailor and Flatley before diving in at the corner for a miraculous score. O'Gara kicked the conversion and suddenly Ireland were only a point behind.

Australia seemed to find an extra gear and hammered the Irish line but the green defensive wall held firm until referee Paddy O'Brien penalised their exhausted backs for offside. Flatley coolly knocked over another penalty to take the lead out to four points.

With an hour gone, Ireland hacked a loose ball up-field and forced a penalty when the Australian defence prevented it from being released. O'Driscoll took a tap kick and unleashed the three-quarters but Shane Horgan knocked O'Gara's cross-field kick on and Keith Wood's touchdown was disallowed. Wood and Keith Gleeson were also denied tries by last-ditch tackles but O'Driscoll ensured Ireland came away with three points after

break down the Australian defence.

Both sides then enjoyed prolonged phases of possession and it was Ireland who eventually won a penalty. O'Gara knocked over an easy three-pointer and cut the deficit to five. Ireland continued applying pressure and another expansive midfield move almost ended with Denis Hickie scoring. The game opened up as both teams tired but Stephen Larkham failed to deliver a crucial pass after a 50-metre move and the half ended with Australia leading by five.

In the first two minutes of the second period, Brian O'Driscoll conceded a pen-

dropping a goal. Both sides kept up an incredible pace for the last 10 minutes but Australia withstood a late barrage to hold on for a one-point win.

Ireland had acquitted themselves well so it was something of a disappointment when they were soundly beaten by the French in the quarter-final. Something had to be done to address the slide. The formation of a Celtic League and the decision to turn the four big provincial sides into club teams was seen as a long-term solution and it began to pay dividends in the first decade of professionalism. Stars like Brian O'Driscoll, Keith Wood and Paul O'Connell emerged from the amateur era to drag Irish rugby from the depths of despair to domestic and international silverware.

Ireland may have lost to the French again in the 2004 Six Nations but the green shoots of recovery blossomed with a long-awaited Triple Crown. England's world ranking had plummeted after their heroics in 2003 so the stage was set for Ireland to assume the unofficial mantle of champions of the northern hemisphere. A Welsh Grand Slam in 2005 momentarily halted their progress but Ireland recorded back-to-back Triple Crowns in 2006 and 2007.

So it came as another surprise when they failed to live up to expectation at the World Cup later in the year. Their hangover continued into 2008 as the Irish only just managed to beat Italy and Scotland, but their fortunes were about to change.

France were first up at Croke Park in Dublin and 79,000 fans were treated to a rampant Ireland who ran in three tries, all of which were converted by Ronan O'Gara. He also added three penalties to seal a 30-21 victory. Ireland ran in five more tries to demolish Italy 38-9 in Rome, and they then squeezed past England by a point after a tense and brutal match in Dublin. Scotland were dispatched in Edinburgh to set up a winner-takes-all encounter with the Welsh at the Millennium Stadium.

The hosts needed to win by 13 points to retain their title so they targeted O'Gara from the whistle. When Ryan Jones caught the fly-half with a mischievous trip in the opening minute, Donncha O'Callaghan confronted the opposing captain and referee Wayne Barnes had to intervene. O'Gara missed the resulting penalty but they almost scored moments later when Gordon D'Arcy broke the first line of defence only for Gavin Henson to tackle Luke

ABOVE Paul O'Connell secures lineout ball against Argentina in 2007

half-hour mark before either side scored.

Stephen Jones finally kicked a penalty, and he doubled the hosts' advantage with a second a minute before the break after Luke Fitzgerald blocked the Welsh defence from tackling O'Gara.

Declan Kidney's halftime team talk did the trick and Ireland began the second half with far more purpose. Tommy Bowe collected O'Driscoll's pass and then O'Gara put up another Garryowen that Mark Jones tried to mark. However, he couldn't stop himself stepping into touch and this gave Ireland a platform for their forwards to drive at the Welsh line. O'Driscoll finally managed to dive over from close range after several phases camped on the Welsh line. Two minutes later, Bowe added a second when he collected O'Gara's delicate chip and beat Shane Williams to score under the posts. O'Gara's two conversions gave the visitors a 14-6 lead but it was too early to be thinking of the Grand Slam.

Wales were given a lifeline when O'Callaghan retaliated against Mike Phillips after the scrum-half had knocked on. Stephen Jones cut the Irish lead to five from the penalty, although the ball deflected off one of the uprights. Tom Shanklin almost levelled the match two

Fitzgerald. O'Gara pumped a high crossfield kick towards Shane Williams but Henson eventually recovered the loose ball and relieved the pressure with a huge clearance. Ireland came again and forced a five-metre scrum but still Wales withstood the pressure and it took until the

minutes later but Brian O'Driscoll saved the day with a last-ditch tackle. Bowe could have extended the Irish lead but he knocked on over the line when trying to out-jump Williams for a high ball.

Irish nerves reached breaking point when they gave Jones another penalty, and Warren Gatland then tried to unset-

BELOW Brian O'Driscoll leads the celebrations after Ireland's historic 2009 Grand Slam

INTRODUCTION

BELOW Australia take on Ireland at the 2011 World Cup

OPPOSITE Ireland celebrate winning the 2014 Six Nations Championship

tle the Irish lineout by throwing on Luke Charteris for Ian Gough and Huw Bennett for Matthew Rees as the game entered the final quarter.

Gavin Henson missed a penalty with 12 minutes to go but Stephen Jones dropped a goal to give Wales a one-point lead with only four minutes left. The Ireland of old might have panicked and blown their chance of glory but the men in green won good lineout ball and span the ball to O'Gara to deliver the coup de grace. He duly dropped the goal and the Irish finally began to believe. It could all have gone wrong at the last minute had Jones's long-range effort not fallen short, but it was Irish eyes that were finally smiling after 61 years without a Grand Slam.

The side struggled to reach the same heights in 2010 and 2011 but they finally avenged previous World Cup defeats to Australia by beating the Wallabies in yet another epic pool match. Unfortunately, they then came up against a resurgent Wales in the quarter-final. Their progress continued with another Six Nations Championship in 2014 – only a narrow 13-10

loss to England denied them a Grand Slam – and superb wins over South Africa and Australia in the autumn international series. They also began the 2015 Six Nations in top form, winning their first three matches, but a narrow loss to Wales denied them a Grand Slam in World Cup year, although they did win the championship on points difference from England and Wales.

With a squad depleted by injury, Ireland had a Six Nations to forget in 2016 winning only two matches in the tournament. They narrowly lost a three-match tour of South Africa but in the Autumn made history when they defeated the All Blacks for the first time in 111 years in Chicago – ending New Zealand's record-breaking streak of 18 Test match wins.

Ireland came second in the 2017 Six Nations and moved to third in the world rankings following their biggest ever win over South Africa, 38-3, in November. They went up to second in the world after winning the 2018 Six Nations with a Grand Slam.

Supporters witnessed a shocking collapse of form in the 2019 Six Nations by the defending champions including an abject display against Wales which ended in a 7-25 loss – a last-gasp try by replacement half-back Jordan Larmour salvaging some points and pride. Ireland was also defeated by hosts Japan in the Rugby World Cup – the biggest upset of the tournament.

It was though the only time in the history of the national team that they reached number one in the world rankings – albeit that five nations held the title at some point during the year!

In their 145th anniversary year, the 2020 Six Nations saw Ireland beat Scotland and Wales before being swept aside by England at Twickenham. The season came to a premature end when the coronavirus pandemic caused the cancellation of worldwide sport from March onwards. While the seedings for the Rugby World Cup 2023 are announced some three years out from the tournament, it is expected that Ireland will be amongst the favourites for at least a quarter-final appearance in France.

They defeated the All Blacks for the first time in 111 years in Chicago – ending New Zealand's record-breaking streak of 18 Test match wins.

Best

Rory Best was raised on the family farm in the village of Poyntzpass on the border between County Down and County Armagh. He graduated from Portadown College and studied agriculture at Newcastle University. While in the northeast, he joined the Newcastle Falcons Rugby Academy but then returned to Northern Ireland to captain the Belfast Harlequins. The club's success led to him being offered a contract with Ulster in 2004 and he made his debut in the Celtic League the following season.

Name: Rory Best
Born: 15th August 1982, Craigavon, Northern Ireland
Position: Hooker
Height: 5'11" (1.80m)
Weight: 243lbs (110kg)
International career: 2005 - 2019
International caps: 124
International points: 60
Honours: Six Nations Triple Crown (2006, 2007, 2009, 2018), Six Nations Grand Slam (2009, 2018), Six Nations Championship (2009, 2014, 2015, 2018)

He was called up for the national team for the autumn international series later in the year, and he came on as a replacement during Ireland's match against an All Black side that had put the Lions to the sword in the summer. New Zealand had already demolished Wales by 38 points in Cardiff and they ran in five tries to crush Ireland by the same margin in Dublin (45-7).

He and his brother, Simon, were retained in the squad for the 2006 Six Nations but Rory wasn't used in the first two matches against Italy and France. He came on towards the end of Ireland's emphatic 31-5 victory over Wales and was used again the following week in a tight win over Scotland. Best then helped Ireland to a historic Triple Crown as the Irish beat England at Twickenham by four points. But for a loss against France, they might have

BEST

RIGHT Rory Best playing for Ireland at the Rugby World Cup 2015

registered a Grand Slam in his first full season.

Best had to share the number-two jersey with Jerry Flannery but he was the first-choice hooker for Ireland's next Triple Crown the following year. Having shown such promise, Ireland were inexplicably poor at the 2007 Rugby World Cup and failed to qualify from their group, although Best did score a try in a narrow win over minnows Georgia. The slump in form continued into the 2008 Six Nations and Ireland could only beat Scotland and Italy.

When Eddie O'Sullivan resigned as manager, Declan Kidney was drafted in to replace him and the impact was immediate: the side began the 2009 tournament with a nine-point win over France at Croke Park, and they followed it up with victory over Italy, a one-point win over England and another narrow victory over Scotland at Murrayfield. The championship would therefore be decided in the final game against Wales in Cardiff. Best and the Irish pack were immense but when Stephen Jones dropped a goal with four minutes left, Wales led by a point and the dream seemed dead. But the 61-year-wait for a Grand Slam was finally over when Ronan O'Gara dropped a goal with only seconds on the clock.

Best was named captain for the sub- sequent tour of North America and he helped Ireland to four straight pool wins at the 2011 World Cup, including a magnificent victory over the Wallabies. He also scored a try against the USA but was rested for the Russia match. Ireland were eventually beaten by Wales in the quarter-final.

With Brian O'Driscoll retiring and Paul O'Connell injured, Best was again named captain for the 2012 Six Nations. He scored a try against Scotland but the Irish could only finish mid-table, although he was later selected for the 2013 British & Irish Lions tour of Australia. He was also ever-present in the championship-winning side for the 2014 Six Nations, and only a narrow loss to England denied him a second Grand Slam. He missed out on another Grand Slam in 2015 after a narrow loss to Wales, but a big win over Scotland on the last day of the championship secured the Six Nations title on points difference from England and Wales.

Best continued as Ireland captain for the 2016 Six Nations and in November became the country's fifth centurion, gaining his 100th cap in a test match against Australia in Dublin. He was selected for the Lions for the second time on the 2017 series in New Zealand and received an OBE while on tour for services to rugby.

He led the team to an historic third Grand Slam and Triple Crown in 2018, winning the Six Nations by defeating England at Twickenham on St. Patrick's Day!

He announced in April 2019 that he would retire from professional rugby after the Rugby World Cup in Japan and played his final test in October when Ireland lost to New Zealand in the quarter-finals receiving a standing ovation from the crowd as he departed the field. He was the most-capped forward to have ever played for Ireland.

Bowe

Tommy Bowe went to The Royal School in Armagh and swapped from fullback to wing having been called up for the national Under-21 side. An accomplished all-round athlete, he also played Gaelic Football to a high standard. He graduated from Queen's University in Belfast and joined the city's Harlequins side before being named Young Irish Player of the Year in 2003.

He soon graduated to the Ulster squad but then signed for the Ospreys and promptly scored a record four tries in a single European Cup game against Treviso. His outstanding club form saw him selected for Ireland for their match against the USA in the 2004 autumn series. He scored a try on debut and gained valuable international experience on a subsequent tour of Japan. He scored another try against Italy in the opening match of the 2006 Six Nations but the side performed poorly against France and he was dropped. The side then rallied and secured a Triple Crown.

He regained his form and helped Ireland to a ninth Triple Crown in 2007 but he was a surprise omission from the World Cup squad later in the year. The side embarrassed themselves, however, and failed to qualify for the quarter-finals. He wasn't recalled until the third match of the 2008 Six Nations and he reminded the selectors what they'd been missing when he scored a brace of tries against Scotland.

The Irish lost three games but regrouped for 2009 and Bowe scored tries against Italy and then Wales in the championship decider in Cardiff. Ireland looked to have blown the Grand Slam when Stephen Jones dropped a late goal but Ronan O'Gara replied for the Irish with one of his own in the last minute.

Bowe continued his great form with two tries against England in the 2010 championship and he was voted the player of the tournament. Ireland underperformed at the 2011 World Cup but Bowe was on sparkling form in the 2012 Six Nations and ran in five tries in Ireland's first three matches. He was called up to the 2013 Lions tour of Australia and he played in two of the Tests. The Lions won the series and made up for the disappointment of the 2009 tour of South Africa. He played in three matches of the 2015 Six Nations including a big win over Scotland on the last day of the championship which secured the Six Nations title on points difference from England and Wales.

The versatile and devastating three-quarter finished with 69 caps and 30 international tries, second only to Brian O'Driscoll with 46 tries. He somewhat uniquely announced his retirement from rugby at the end of the 2018 season in a poem on twitter:

LEFT Tommy Bowe turns out for the Ospreys

BELOW Bowe (right) with Osprey team-mate Gavin Henson

Name: Thomas John Bowe
Born: 22nd February 1984, County Monaghan, Ireland
Position: Wing / Centre
Height: 6'3" (1.91m)
Weight: 225lbs (102kg)
International career: 2004 - 2017
International caps: 69
International points: 150
Honours: Six Nations Triple Crown (2006, 2007), Six Nations Grand Slam (2009), Lions Tour Winner (2013), Six Nations Championship (2009, 2014, 2015)

"I've spent most of my career in Belfast,
At first George said I wasn't very fast,
I eventually found my gears,
Had some incredible years,
But it's time to tell you - this is my last! "

Campbell

Hamstring problems hampered Ollie Campbell's early career but he still made an impression at Belvedere College and helped his side to the Leinster Schools Senior Cup in 1971 and 1972. He first played for Ireland aged 21 in 1976 but he didn't play again until 1979, although he would go on to score 217 points in just 22 internationals.

He enjoyed a successful trip to Australia with the national side in 1979 and set an Irish record with 19 points against the hosts in Brisbane and 60 points overall on the tour. This proved to be the springboard to success with the Lions because he was selected for the 1980 trip to South Africa. He played in three Tests having recovered from yet more hamstring troubles, with his first action coming as a replacement during the second Test in Bloemfontein.

Campbell started the

third and fourth Tests and was the Lions' leading points' scorer on the tour. His accuracy with the boot and reliable distribution saw him selected again for the 1983 tour to New Zealand but the side was not particularly strong and he only won one of his seven Tests for the tourists. Despite this, Campbell was named one of the New *Zealand Rugby Almanac's* five players of the year.

His defining moment was helping Ireland to their first Triple Crown in 33 years during the 1982 Five Nations. He kicked a record six penalties and a drop-goal against Scotland at Lansdowne Road in the championship decider, and they took a share of the title the following year.

Name: Seamus Oliver 'Ollie' Campbell
Born: 5th March 1954, Dublin
Position: Fly-half
Height: 5'10" (1.78m)
Weight: 169lbs (77kg)
International career: 1976 - 1984
International caps: 29
International points: 243
Honours: Five Nations Triple Crown (1982), Five Nations Championship (1983)

Campbell retired from international rugby after Ireland's 9-18 loss to Wales in 1984 and from all rugby two years later. He has since worked as a company director in the family clothing business.

BELOW Campbell shows no signs of his hamstring troubles as he launches a kick

Crawford

Ernie Crawford was another talented all-rounder who could have chosen football over rugby having represented Cliftonville and Malone respectively. He moved to Dublin but, despite being named captain of Lansdowne RFC, he still played football for Bohemians and couldn't decide where his allegiance lay. His mind was made up for him in 1920 when he was selected for the national team for a Five Nations match against England in Dublin. This was the first championship after the Great War and all the home unions had lost players in the trenches.

Ireland had been particularly badly affected and they lost a tight match by three points. They were then thumped by Scotland in Edinburgh (19-0) and Wales in Cardiff (28-4). Their last match in the championship was another narrow loss to France in Dublin. Ireland avenged the defeat to Scotland the following year but they still finished

Crawford played his last international against Wales at the denouement of the 1927 championship. Ireland won the match in Dublin comfortably...

bottom of the table. They wouldn't register two championship wins until 1924, by which time Crawford had already captained the side against the touring All Blacks.

The upsurge in Irish fortunes between 1924 and 1927 was doubtless linked to Crawford leading the team, and they finished second in the 1925 Five Nations, albeit behind Scotland's Grand Slam winners. Having beaten France 11-0, England by four points (their first win over the English for 15 years) and Scotland by three, Ireland were on course for a Grand Slam of their own in 1926 but they were beaten 11-8 by the Welsh in Cardiff and had to settle for a share of the title with the Scots.

Crawford played his last international against Wales at the denouement of the 1927 championship. Ireland won the match in Dublin comfortably but a two-point defeat to England earlier in the tournament again denied them a Grand Slam (the title was shared with Scotland once more).

This multi-talented star made the squad for Ireland's 1924 Olympic football team and was serving as a rugby selector when Ireland finally completed the elusive Grand Slam under Jack Kyle in 1948.

Name: William Ernest 'Ernie' Crawford
Born: 17th November 1891, Belfast, Northern Ireland
Died: 12th January 1959
Position: Fullback
International career: 1920 - 1927
International caps: 30
International points: 18
Honours: Five Nations Championship (1926, 1927)

LEFT The legendary Ernie Crawford

Clohessy

Although Peter Clohessy's international trophy cabinet is bare, 'The Claw' is a living legend as one of the hardest players ever to have played for Ireland.

He made his name as part of the terrifying Young Munster 'Cookie Monsters' pack of the early 1990s, three of whom featured in the Munster side that stunned Australia at Musgrave Park in 1992. Knowing they could not hope to match the world champions in terms of skill, Munster set out to 'sow it into them' and Clohessy was chief henchman, to the point of being singled out afterwards by furious Wallabies coach Bob Dwyer, who labelled the fearsome prop an "animal".

He made his Ireland debut against France in February

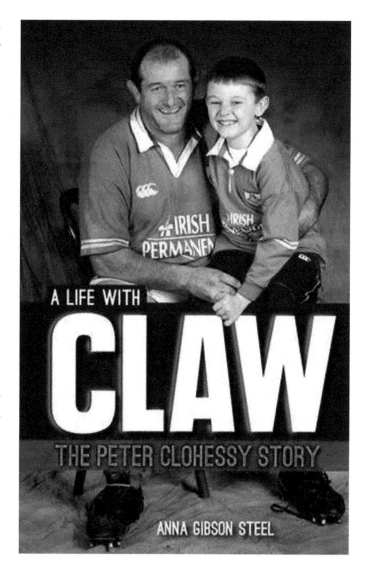

A LIFE WITH **CLAW** THE PETER CLOHESSY STORY

ANNA GIBSON STEEL

'The Claw' never lost his ruthless edge, nor his reputation as one of the toughest of the tough

1993 in the Five Nations Championship while his first try for his country came against Australia in June 1994. His bad boy reputation grew when he was suspended for stamping on St Mary's Steve Jameson during an AIL match and he was again suspended for the same offence against France's Olivier Roumat in Parc des Princes in 1996.

In the infamous 'Battle of Pretoria' against South Africa in 1998, 'The Claw' and fellow hardman Trevor Brennan were bought off the bench to ensure that even though the match was irretrievably lost, Ireland would go down fighting.

Clohessy missed the 1995 Rugby World Cup but was selected for Ireland's squad for the 1999 tournament. He was considered desperately unlucky not to be picked for the 1993 British Lions tour to New Zealand and only didn't tour with the 1997 Lions because of injury (Paul Wallace took his place and made the Test team).

Hugely popular with the Irish fans, Clohessy's disciplinary issues sometimes took attention away from the fact that he was one hell of a rugby player.

When professionalism kicked in, Clohessy cleaned up his act, reinvented himself as a loosehead and ended up with 54 caps for Ireland but 'The Claw' never lost his ruthless edge, nor his reputation as one of the toughest of the tough – they say in Limerick mothers keep his picture on the mantelpiece to keep the kids away from the fire.

Name: Peter Clohessy
Born: 22nd March 1966
Limerick, Ireland
Position: Prop
Height: 5'11" (1.80m)
Weight: 234lbs (106kg)
International career: 1993-2002
International caps: 54
International points: 20

D'Arcy

Gordon D'Arcy showed promise as a fullback while at Clongowes Wood School but he was a surprise selection for the national team when Warren Gatland's men toured South Africa in 1998. As he was still studying, he turned Gatland down and didn't make his debut until Ireland's World Cup pool match against Romania in 1999.

His career faltered when he fell out with the domestic coaches at Leinster and he almost retired after being sidelined for the next three years. He returned to the national team for Ireland's match against Fiji in the 2002 autumn internationals but he only made three appearances as a sub the following year and missed out on the World Cup. With the

RIGHT Gordon D'Arcy warms up for the Six Nations clash with Wales in 2014

country's best players away in Australia, D'Arcy produced the finest rugby of his career and he continued his resurgence when he switched to outside centre in place of the injured Brian O'Driscoll.

D'Arcy was inspirational in the 2004 Six Nations as the Irish recovered from a poor opening match against France to claim a Triple Crown and second place in the championship. When O'Driscoll returned, the selectors shifted him to inside centre as D'Arcy was now seen as indispensible. The pair combined beautifully throughout the championship and varied the traditional centre roles (inside made the hard yards while outside made the breaks), none more

Name: Gordon William D'Arcy
Born: 10th February 1980, County Wexford, Ireland
Position: Inside Centre
Height: 5'11" (1.80m)
Weight: 200lbs (91kg)
International career: 1999 - 2015
International caps: 82
International points: 35
Honours: Six Nations Triple Crown (2004, 2006, 2007), Six Nations Grand Slam (2009)

so than in a seminal encounter against England at Twickenham that Ireland won by six points. D'Arcy then scored a brace against Scotland and was voted man of the tournament to cap a remarkable comeback to international rugby.

He was selected for the disastrous 2005 Lions tour to New Zealand and there were fears that his previous year might have been the highlight of his career. He proved his consistency at the highest level by beating the most defenders in the 2006 Six Nations and he helped Ireland to rare victories over South Africa and Australia in the autumn. He was again nominated as player of the tournament after the 2007 Six Nations but the subsequent World Cup was a disaster.

Ireland rebuilt the side around the centre pairing of O'Driscoll and D'Arcy and they won a Grand Slam in 2009. Both scored tries against France and, largely due to D'Arcy's vision and distribution, O'Driscoll was top try-scorer in the tournament with five. He toured again with the 2009 Lions in South Africa, and he and O'Driscoll broke Will Carling and Jeremy Guscott's world record centre partnership (45 appearances) in Ireland's epic win over Australia at the 2011 World Cup.

Davidson

Jeremy Davidson was a giant but mobile second-row who began his club career with Dungannon before moving to London Irish and then Castres Olympique. He made his Test debut in Ireland's 44-8 annihilation of Fiji at Lansdowne Road in 1995. He was then selected for the 1997 Lions' tour to South Africa and was omnipresent in the engine room. His partnership with Martin Johnson was one of the reasons the Springboks got no change from the Lions pack, and he was equally proficient at the set-piece to deny the hosts lineout ball. Davidson was voted the players' player of the tour.

In 1999 he played three matches for Ireland at the World Cup and made his final appearance in the green jersey at Murrayfield in 2001, although Ireland were hammered 32-10. He was selected for the Lions tour of Australia later that year but couldn't reach the heights of South Africa and didn't play in any of the Tests.

...He was then selected for the 1997 Lions' tour to South Africa and was omnipresent in the engine room. His partnership with Martin Johnson was one of the reasons the Springboks got no change from the Lions pack.

He finished his career with 32 Irish caps after aggravating an old injury and has since enjoyed stints as Director of Rugby at Dungannon and as a coach at Castres. In 2009 he joined the coaching staff at Ulster. Two years later, he returned to France to coach Aurillac in the second-tier of the domestic leagues. He proved so popular at the club that he was linked with a coaching role at Clermont but he missed out to Jono Gibbes as the Kiwi lock had won three Heineken Cups with Leinster. He currently coaches Brive whom he helped win promotion to the top tier of French rugby.

LEFT Jeremy Davidson takes a breath during a brief break in play

Name: Jeremy Davidson
Born: 28th April 1974, Belfast
Position: Lock
Height: 6'6" (1.98m)
Weight: 252lbs (115kg)
International career: 1995 - 2001
International caps: 32
International points: 0
Honours: Lions Tour Winner (1997)

He finished his career with 32 Irish caps after aggravating an old injury and has since enjoyed stints as Director of Rugby at Dungannon and as a coach at Brive.

Dawson

Ronnie Dawson was schooled at St Andrew's College in Dublin and later at the Dublin Institute of Technology. He qualified as an architect and played his club rugby with Wanderers FC from 1950, although he still worked fulltime for the Bank of Ireland. He was also a Leinster stalwart on the provincial stage, playing 28 times between 1958 and 1964.

His international debut also came in 1958 in a match against Australia. Ireland won and Dawson was promoted to captain for the next 11 games, which included the 1961 tour to South Africa. They only played one Test, which Ireland lost comfortably, but the Irish then won their five remaining matches against the provincial sides.

Dawson's strong leadership and qual-

RIGHT Ronnie Dawson leads the Lions out against the All Blacks in 1959

He was rewarded for his service to the game in 2004 when he was presented with the IRB's Vernon Pugh Award. In 2013, Dawson was inducted into the IRB Hall of Fame.

ity at the set-piece and breakdown saw him selected as captain for the 1959 Lions tour to Australia, New Zealand and Canada. His six Tests in the role wasn't equalled until Martin Johnson led the team for all three Tests in South Africa in 1997 and Australia four years later. Dawson's Lions kicked off the tour with two big wins against Australia but they narrowly lost the first two Tests against the All Blacks. The third Test ended in a 14-point defeat, although the Lions finally roared in Auckland and won the last match on this leg of the tour 9-6. They also won both of their matches in Canada on their way home.

Dawson was unavailable for the 1962 side but did return to duty with the Lions as assistant manager for the 1968 tour to South Africa, and he has also held a position on the selection committee.

He retired from international rugby in 1965 with 27 Ireland caps, six for the Lions and a reputation for developing new coaching techniques. He subsequently became a successful rugby administrator and was a dedicated Home Union Committee member for more than 20 years. He was rewarded for his service to the game in 2004 when he was presented with the IRB's Vernon Pugh Award. In 2013, Dawson was inducted into the IRB Hall of Fame.

Name: Alfred Ronald 'Ronnie' Dawson
Born: 5th June 1932, Dublin
Position: Hooker
Height: 5'11" (1.80m)
Weight: 176lbs (80kg)
International career: 1958 - 1965
International caps: 33
International points: 6
Honours: British Lions Captain (1959)

Dempsey

Girvan Dempsey went to Terenure College before graduating to the National College of Ireland. He often played for Leinster as a utility back and was eventually called up to the national team for an autumn international against Romania. He came on as a replacement and scored two tries in an entertaining 53-35 win at Lansdowne Road.

He was used mainly from the bench over the next two years but he was the first-choice fullback for the 2003 World

Cup in Australia. Dempsey started every match of the campaign and scored a try in a 64-7 demolition of Namibia. A narrow win over Argentina meant their final group game against the host nation would decide who topped the pool. In yet another epic Ireland-Australia World Cup clash, the Australians squeezed home by a point and left Ireland to face France in the quarter-final. The Irish scored three tries through Kevin Maggs and Brian O'Driscoll but the French ran in four and also kicked five penalties.

Dempsey was on top form during the 2004 Six Nations and his try against England at Twickenham helped Ireland to a first Triple Crown in 20 years. He earned his 50th cap on the difficult sum-mer tour of South Africa but the Irish avenged their two Test defeats during a thrilling autumn international series in which they also recorded wins over the United States and Argentina.

Ireland beat Italy, thumped Scotland and edged past England in their first three fixtures of the 2005 Six Nations but the wheels came off against France and Wales and they could only finish the championship in third place. But for a 12-point defeat to France in Paris, Ireland might have secured an elusive Grand Slam in 2006 but they had to make do with another Triple Crown.

They lost again in the corresponding fixture the following year – this time by an agonising three points – but Dempsey was on the score-sheet once more when he crossed the whitewash against England in a 43-13 drubbing for the visitors at Croke Park. Scotland put up a brave fight in Edinburgh but the Irish secured a third Triple Crown in four years with a one-point win. Dempsey then capped a superb tournament with a brace of tries against Italy in Ireland's last match.

He retired from international rugby in 2008 and from all rugby when Leinster were eliminated from the 2009-10 Heineken Cup.

LEFT Shane Byrne congratulates Girvan Dempsey on his try against England in 2004

Name: Girvan Dempsey
Born: 2nd October 1975, Dublin, Ireland
Position: Fullback
Height: 6'0" (1.83m)
Weight: 201lbs (91kg)
International career: 1998 - 2008
International caps: 82
International points: 95
Honours: Six Nations Triple Crown (2004, 2006, 2007)

Duggan

Willie Duggan was an old-school forward who played hard and partied hard. He was first capped by Ireland for their home match against England in the 1975 Five Nations, which the hosts won 12-9 at Lansdowne Road despite being behind at halftime. The Irish lost to Scotland and were thumped by a Wales in their pomp, but they hammered France 25-6 and finished the season mid-table.

The Irish were poor for the next few years but the revival began in England's Grand Slam year of 1980 when they beat Scotland and Wales and only lost narrowly to the French. Duggan was now in his prime and he was promoted to captain before the glorious Triple Crown season of 1982 (the French scuppered their Grand Slam aspirations in the final match of the championship).

Duggan went on to appear 41 times for his country and he only retired after Ireland's dismal showing in 1984 when they failed to win a single game.

Duggan was selected for the 1977 Lions tour to New Zealand as he was one of the few forwards who enjoyed genuine respect from the Kiwi players.

His combative nature saw him become the first Irishman sent off during a Five Nations international (against Wales in 1977), although he didn't view the incident as seriously as those watching: "The referee politely asked me if I minded leaving the field, to which I replied, 'No problem, I'm buggered anyway.'"

Duggan was selected for the 1977 Lions tour to New Zealand as he was one of the few forwards who enjoyed genuine respect from the Kiwi players. His training methods may have left a little to be desired – he once handed the referee his cigarette as he took the field – but there's no doubting his commitment, work ethic and ferociousness in the tackle.

The charismatic Duggan remained a huge supporter of the game and was one of Ireland's most revered and loved rugby players right up until his death from an aneurysm at his home in Dunmore, just outside Kilkenny city, in August 2017.

LEFT Willie Duggan in action for the Lions

BELOW The Lansdowne Road Stadium where Duggan made his debut for Ireland in the 1975 Five Nations against England.

Name: William Patrick Duggan
Born: 12th March 1950
Died: 28th August 2017
Position: Number 8
Height: 6'4" (1.93m)
Weight: 220lbs (100kg)
International career: 1975 - 1984
International caps: 45
International points: 8
Honours: Five Nations Championship and Triple Crown (1982)

Earls

RIGHT Keith Earls playing for Ireland in the Rugby World Cup 2015 game against Canada at Millennium Stadium in Cardiff.

A prodigal talent with explosive pace, Keith Earls first broke onto the rugby scene when he played for Munster against Ospreys aged 19. Within a couple of years, he won his first Irish cap against Canada in November 2008 and scored a try with his first touch of the ball!

Incredibly, just two years after his first senior match for Munster he was selected as part of the 2009 British and Irish Lions tour to South Africa although he did not win a full cap on the tour despite some impressive try-scoring performances in several tour matches. He played in all of Ireland's Six Nations Championship games in 2010 and 2011 as well as in that year's Rugby World Cup where he finished the tournament as Ireland's top try scorer with five tries – his last coming in the quarter-final defeat at the hands of Wales.

His reputation continued to grow over the following years' Six Nations Championships leading to the 2015

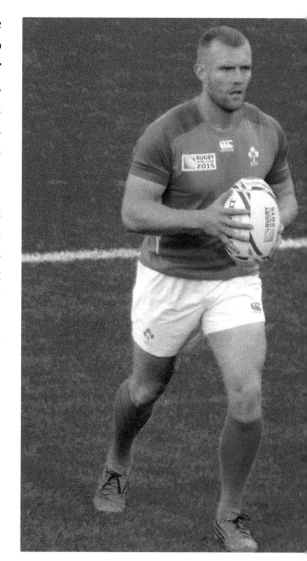

Rugby World Cup in which his three tries in two of the opening pool matches took him past Brian O'Driscoll as Ireland's leading try-scorer in RWC history.

In June 2016, he started on the wing for Ireland in their first ever win over the Springboks on South African soil. However, his two-week suspension as a result of red card he received against Glasgow Warriors meant that he missed Ireland's first-ever victory against the All Blacks in Chicago just a few months later that year.

Earls scored nine tries over the course of the international season in 2017 setting a new record for Ireland, which he followed by playing in every game for Ireland as they won a Grand Slam in the 2018 Six Nations.

He won the Players' Player of the Year Award at the 2018 Rugby Players Ireland Awards in May of that year becoming the fourth Munster player in a row to win the trophy after O'Connell, Stander and Murray. To the club's relief, he signed a new three-year deal with Munster up to the end of June 2021.

He started in all three tests in Ireland's historic 2-1 series victory against Australia and in the Autumn Tests played in the country's famous 16-9 win over New Zealand - a victory that was his first ever against the All Blacks and Ireland's first win in Dublin against New Zealand.

He started all five games in the 2019 Six Nations, was selected for the Ireland squad for the 2019 Rugby World Cup where the national side suffered the ignomy of losing to unfancied hosts Japan before being dumped out of the tournament in the knock out stage by New Zealand.

Despite his ailing knees Earls is still one of the quickest players in European rugby and his versatility means he can play at centre as well as any of the back three positions. The "fire in the belly ", as he puts it, still burns.

Name: Keith Gerard Earls
Born: 2nd October 1987
Moyross, Limerick, Ireland
Position: Centre, fullback, wing
Height: 5'10" (1.78m)
Weight: 192lbs (87kg)
International career: 2008 – present
International caps: 84
International points: 150
Honours: Six Nations Grand Slam (2018)

Easterby

Simon Easterby was educated at Ampleforth College in Yorkshire. He played for Leeds Carnegie until 1999 but then joined Llanelli for the next four years. This coincided with a barren time for Irish rugby but Simon and his brother, Guy, made their debuts for the national team in 2000.

Easterby won his first game against Scotland but it took a couple of seasons before he became a focal point in the Irish back row alongside Anthony Foley. Ireland showed promise in the Six Nations campaign and were reasonably competitive on their summer tour of the Americas – Easterby scored two tries in an 83-3 annihilation of the USA but the side lost to Argentina and could only draw with Canada – and he picked up an injury at the end of the year, thereby missing Ireland's impressive showing in the 2001 Six Nations.

Ireland humiliated a woeful Wales 54-10 in the first game of the 2002 Six Nations but they were then soundly beaten by England. Easterby scored in a big win over Scotland, and another win over Italy kept their championship hopes alive. A crushing defeat to France on the final weekend almost cost Easterby his place and he was eventually dropped after the autumn internationals.

He returned to the fold for the 2003 summer tour of the Pacific Islands and was ever-present in the side for that year's World Cup, which ended in a heavy quarter-final defeat to France. Ireland bounced back and secured a Triple Crown in 2004 but England and France were still suffering from their exertions at the World Cup and had lost many top players to retirement. Ireland continued to improve, although they couldn't prevent a Welsh Grand Slam in 2005.

Easterby wasn't initially selected to tour with the Lions in New Zealand later in the year but Lawrence Dallaglio picked up an injury so he joined the squad. He missed the first Test but scored a try in a losing cause in the second and retained his place for the third Test in Auckland.

The All Blacks had already won the series and they whitewashed the Lions with a comprehensive 38-19 win.

Name: Simon Easterby
Born: 21st July 1975, Harrogate, England
Position: Flanker
Height: 6'4" (1.93m)
Weight: 220lbs (100kg)
International career: 2000 - 2008
International caps: 67
International points: 45
Honours: Triple Crown (2004, 2006, 2007)

Easterby helped the national side to an impressive Triple Crown in 2006 and another in 2007, although they missed out on both championships to France on points difference. He scored another try against Italy in the 2007 Six Nations but retired from international rugby after two narrow defeats and then a heavy loss to England in the last match of the 2008 championship.

He picked up a serious knee injury playing for the Scarlets in 2010 and retired from the domestic game. He immediately took up a position as the side's defensive coach and he became the national team's forwards' coach in 2014.

Elwood

Eric Elwood played for Galwegians and Lansdowne before being selected for the Barbarians in their end-of-season encounter with the touring All Blacks in 1993. New Zealand won the match 25-12 but Elwood at fly-half kicked all the Barbarians' points. He wasn't selected for the Irish national squad for another two years but he eventually made his debut in the Five Nations. Ireland lost to England and Scotland, and Elwood's first international points – a penalty against France – were also in vain as the French ran riot in Dublin.

Ireland came out firing against New Zealand in the pool stages of the 1995 World Cup and Elwood converted two of their tries, but the All Blacks had a secret weapon in the form of Jonah Lomu and Ireland were eventually beaten comfortably. Elwood returned for the decisive match against Wales and chipped in with another 11 points as Ireland sneaked home 24-23. He then kicked all of Ireland's 12 points in a heavy quarter-final loss to France.

Elwood's precise tactical kicking, slick distribution and solidity in the tackle made up for a lack of pace.

Elwood's precise tactical kicking, slick distribution and solidity in the tackle made up for a lack of pace, but even he couldn't lift an Irish side suffering in the early years of professionalism and they finished bottom of the 1996 Five Nations. In 1997 he kicked all of Ireland's points against France and England but both matches ended in heavy defeat. Ireland could only manage a narrow win over Wales in Cardiff and again propped up the table. His kicking kept the Irish in several games the following season, but they were whitewashed after suffering three narrow defeats and then a 35-17 drubbing by England.

When David Humphreys took over the kicking duties in the last Five Nations Championship in 1999, Elwood was relegated to the bench and he only made brief appearances as a substitute thereafter. He was selected for the World Cup later that year and kicked 16 points in Ireland's must-win game against Romania. The side then lost to Argentina in a quarter-final playoff and were eliminated. Elwood had come on late in the match but the South Americans shocked the Irish with a four-point win in Lens and Elwood retired immediately afterwards.

He played on with Connacht until 2005 and has continued coaching with the club side where he is now head of the Academy, although this lengthy spell was punctuated with a two-year stint with the national Under-20 side between 2006-07.

LEFT Eric Elwood takes a pot at goal

Name: Eric Elwood
Born: 26th February 1969, Galway, Ireland
Position: Fly-half
Height: 6'0" (1.83m)
Weight: 203lbs (92kg)
International career: 1995 - 2002
International caps: 35
International points: 296
Honours: World Cup Quarter-final (1995)

Foley

Anthony Foley's father was in the Munster side that beat the touring All Blacks 12-0 in 1978 and his sister was an Ireland international so the sport ran in the family. Anthony joined Shannon in 1992 and played in all 48 games for the side that won four consecutive All-Ireland titles. He was promptly called up to the national team for the 1995 Five Nations and scored a try on debut against England, although Jack Rowell's side would win the game comfortably before securing a third Grand Slam in five years. Ireland only managed a single win against Wales in their last match and Foley was selected for the World Cup later in the year.

He only played one match at the tournament, a thrilling 50-28 win over Japan, and Ireland needed a one-point win over Wales to scrape through to the quarter-final. A heavy defeat to France highlighted the deficiencies in Irish rugby and the side struggled to cope in the early years of professionalism. Indeed, over the next five years, Ireland would only win four Five Nations matches.

Foley moved from Shannon to Munster after the World Cup and played in the side's first Heineken Cup match against Swansea in November. It would be a bittersweet tournament for the veteran back-row forward as he was on the losing side in two finals – against Northampton in 2000 and Leicester two years later – but he eventually captained the team to the trophy after a 23-19 win over Biarritz Olympique in 2006.

Foley missed the 1999 Rugby World Cup but Ireland at last rediscovered their form in the 2000 Six Nations. They may have lost their opening match to England but wins against France in Paris, as well as Scotland and Italy, saw them finish third in the championship. The resurgence continued in 2001 and only Scotland denied them a Grand Slam. Foley was then named captain for Ireland's autumn international against Samoa later in the year. He was at the helm the following year for victories over Romania and Georgia, and he travelled to Australia as part of the 2003 World Cup team. He only played in two of the pool matches – a big win over Romania and yet another narrow loss to the hosts – and Ireland exited after a heavy defeat to France in the quarter-final.

He played his final international against Wales in 2005 but continued with Munster for another three years. In 2014, he took over from Rob Penney as head coach of the domestic giants.

He played his final international against Wales in 2005 but continued with Munster for another three years. In 2014, he took over from Rob Penney as head coach but died at a tragically early age of heart failure in his sleep at a hotel in a Paris suburb in October 2016 while preparing for a match against Racing 92, which was subsequently postponed. He was posthumously inducted into the Munster hall of fame during the club's 2018 Rugby Awards.

Name: Anthony Foley
Born: 30th October 1973, Limerick, Ireland
Position: Flanker / Number 8
Height: 6'3" (1.91m)
Weight: 245lbs (111kg)
International career: 1995 - 2005
International caps: 62
International points: 25
Honours: Six Nations Triple Crown (2004)

LEFT A young Anthony Foley in the green of Ireland

Furlong

Tadhg Furlong had less than 20 Ireland caps when he was selected by Warren Gatland for the 2017 British & Irish Lions – but such was the young prop's quality, he started every Test.

He had truly established himself as a key man for Ireland the previous November, and underlined his credentials as a player for New Zealand to fear after a dynamic run saw him brush off tackles from Brodie Retallick and Kieran Read during the historic win over the All Blacks in Chicago.

Furlong made his Lions debut off the bench against the New Zealand Barbarians before starting against the Crusaders and the Maori All Blacks. Impressive front-row performances alongside Mako Vunipola and Jamie George earned the tight-head prop a Test spot as he completed 338 minutes in total during the Tour.

The Irishman was superb in all three Tests, as alongside the two Englishmen the Lions' front row held firm, and Furlong in particular had the measure of his opposite number Joe Moody throughout the Tests.

Furlong came from a farming family in County Wexford and started his playing underage for local club New Ross RFC. He made his senior debut for Leinster Rugby in November 2013 and has helped the club to win the European Rugby Champions Cup in 2018, as well as Pro 14 in 2018 and 2019.

He cemented his reputation as one of the best tightheads in the game with his performances in the 2018 Grand Slam campaign, particularly against England. The good times came to a halt though in the 2019 Rugby World Cup which Furlong described as gut-wrenching.

"It's very hard to put your finger on where it went wrong. We were just off in a small few areas. It's disappointing for the players and the coaching staff. We said goodbye to Joe Schmidt, to Greg Feek, to Mervyn Murphy, to

Name: Tadhg Furlong
Born: 14th November 1992
Wexford, Ireland
Position: Prop
Height: 6'0" (1.83m)
Weight: 269lbs (122kg)
International career: 2015-present
International caps: 47
International points: 25
Honours: Six Nations Grand Slam
(2018)

Enda [McNulty]. It was a bleak time but what can you do? You go back to Leinster and you drive on."

Early on in his career he was branded "The Mayor of Wexford" by Irish Under-20s coach Mike Ruddock, but Furlong wasn't happy with this and created his own nickname as The Jukebox. Asked why, he replied: " Because the hits keep coming!"

LEFT Tadhg Furlong - " The Jukebox ".

Geoghegan

Simon Geoghegan's grandfather may have played in the 1929 All-Ireland hurling final but Simon only qualified to play rugby for the country because his father had been born in Galway. In the days before professionalism, Geoghegan trained as a solicitor but he also turned out for London Irish. He soon forged a reputation as a livewire winger with a great sidestep and ferocious speed over short distances.

He was selected for the national team during the 1991 Five Nations and he scored a try in only his second match, an epic 21-all draw with Wales at the old Cardiff Arms Park. He scored again in a narrow defeat to England the following week and rounded off a superb personal championship with a third try against Scotland. He was one of few players to emerge from the campaign in credit, however. This was a low point in Irish rugby history and a solitary point after the draw with Wales left them joint bottom of the table.

He was picked for the World Cup later in the year and scored a try in a dominant 55-11 win over Zimbabwe. A loss to Scotland pitted them against Australia in the quarter-final. The match was the first of several World Cup classics between the two countries. Ireland had home advantage at Lansdowne Road and they began playing an expansive game. Indiscipline at the breakdown gave Michael Lynagh an early shot at goal, but he missed an easy kick. Australia maintained the pressure but Lynagh, Horan and Campese were held up just short of the Irish line. Campese then took a crash ball in midfield and burst through the cover defence to score his 44th international try.

The Australian backs kept trying the same midfield move and the Irish fell for it again. Referee Jim Fleming disallowed the try, however, because Jason Little hadn't released the ball when half-tackled by Geoghegan in the build-up. The Irish then broke up-field from a scrum. Jim Staples kicked through for

Jack Clarke to chase and he beat Campese to the ball, then popped it inside to flanker Gordon Hamilton and the big back-row forward galloped home from 40 metres. Lansdowne Road erupted as the Irish took a one-point lead with five minutes to play.

The Wallabies didn't panic, however. They used the same midfield move to get position in the Irish 22, and used a similar set play to free Campese on the right-hand side. He couldn't evade Staples's cover tackle but the ball popped up to Lynagh and the fly-half scored in the corner to break Irish hearts.

The Irish didn't win a match in the following Five Nations and 1993 was equally poor, although Geoghegan was tipped to tour with the 1993 Lions. Having been controversially omitted from the squad, Geoghegan lifted his and Irish spirits with a devastating display against England in 1994. He scored a crucial try and then set up a penalty chance with a deft kick and chase that saw Rob Andrew take a crunching hit before failing to release the ball. Elwood kicked the points and Ireland held on to win 13-12.

He managed to score another try against France in 1995 but Ireland's Five Nations campaign only yielded a solitary win over Wales. Geoghegan scored against Japan at the 1995 World Cup but Ireland were well beaten by France in the quarter-final. Although he was only 28, Geoghegan then suffered a career-threatening toe injury. He managed a final international try in a comfortable 30-17 win against the Welsh in 1996 but the injury eventually curtailed his career and he retired at the end of the championship. An adept sidestepper, he was famously described by commentator Bill McLaren as being "Like a mad trout up a burn ".

Name: Simon Patrick Geoghegan
Born: 1st September 1968, Knebworth, England
Position: Wing
Height: 6'0" (1.83m)
Weight: 183lbs (83kg)
International career: 1991 - 1996
International caps: 37
International points: 51
Honours: World Cup Quarter-final (1991, 1995)

Gibson

Former Cambridge University three-quarter Mike Gibson was a rugby perfectionist, but he was good enough to meet the standards he set for himself. He was perhaps the greatest centre in the game's history and his longevity – five Lions tours – proves he could always mix it with the best from the southern hemisphere.

His brilliance lay in the perception and timing of his runs, the anticipation and power of his defence, and the commitment to stay at the top for 15 years and a then-record 81 international appearances (for both the Lions and Ireland). He also played nine times for the Barbarians, although they didn't count as full international caps.

His first two Lions tours gave him valuable experience, and he became the first replacement in top-flight rugby when he came on in the opening Test against South Africa in 1968. With Barry John out injured, Gibson played in 11 of the next 13 matches and didn't disappoint. His

RIGHT Mike Gibson of Ireland and the British Lions

finest hour came on the New Zealand tour in 1971, when he teamed up with John and John Dawes to form arguably the perfect midfield trio.

The host crowds loved his blistering runs and perfectly timed passing. In the second Test it was Gibson's beautiful interplay with JPR Williams and Gerald Davies that sent the latter flying up the wing to score having destroyed the world's best defence in the blink of an eye.

Gibson joined the 1974 tour as a replacement and he displayed a remarkable lack of ego in playing understudy – and passing on his wisdom – to the

Name: Cameron Michael Henderson 'Mike' Gibson, MBE
Born: 3rd December 1942, Belfast, Northern Ireland
Position: Centre
Height: 5'11" (1.80m)
Weight: 178lbs (81kg)
International career: 1964 - 1979
International caps: 81
International points: 112
Honours: Lions Tour Winner (1971, 1974), Five Nations Championship (1973, 1974)

new Test pairing of Ian McGeechan and Dick Milliken. He equalled Willie John McBride's record of five Lions tours in 1977 but injuries prevented him from competing for a Test place. It was a tame end to a brilliant career, although the All Blacks must have been delighted to see the back of him.

When he was inducted in the IRB Hall of Fame in 2011, fellow inductee Syd Millar spoke of the man who "was one of the finest players of his generation, one of the finest players ever to represent Ireland and the British & Irish Lions, and a man who epitomised the ethos of the game and its values". Irish legend Brian O'Driscoll was equally impressed with Gibson's contribution: "At times when Irish rugby wasn't successful, Mike was always the shining light. He played international rugby for 15 years and that speaks volumes. He was a magnificent player and a great ambassador for our game."

His record of 69 Ireland caps stood until it was overtaken by Malcolm O'Kelly in 2005, and his 56 Five Nations appearances remained a record until Ronan O'Gara played his 57th match in 2011.

Hayes

John Hayes was more interested in Gaelic Football and hurling than rugby but by the age of 18 he'd developed into a man of 6'4" and nearly 19 stone. Friends convinced him to take up the sport but he initially played in the second row because of his size. He travelled to New Zealand and, having put on another stone of muscle, decided to move to the front row. He returned to join Shannon but was also picked for Munster and by 1998 he was a formidable scrummager who was surprisingly mobile.

England's pack demolished Ireland in the first match of the 2000 Six Nations so Hayes was drafted in for their second game against Scotland. He successfully anchored the scrum and Ireland ran out easy winners. They also thumped Italy by 47 points but it was a two-point win over France in Paris that cemented his reputation. Brian O'Driscoll may have stolen the headlines with a hat-trick but the pack still had to win enough ball for the backs to win the match. Ireland eventually ran in 17 tries in the championship and finished in third place.

Having been in the international wilderness for much of the past decade, Irish rugby suddenly enjoyed a resurgence, and there can be no doubt that Hayes and O'Driscoll were the catalysts for the team's success. Ireland narrowly missed out on a Grand Slam in 2001 and Hayes wasn't selected for the Lions in Australia. Defeat to both England and France in 2002 couldn't slow their progress and Ireland beat France in 2003 to set up a Grand Slam decider against England. This was England's year, however, and Hayes for once was subdued in the pack.

Ireland suffered a heavy defeat to France in the quarter-final of the World Cup but the side bounced back from another defeat to the same side to claim a Triple Crown in the 2004 Six Nations. Hayes scored his first international try in a thumping 40-13

LEFT John Hayes (left) in action against England

Name: John James Hayes
Born: 2nd November 1973,
Limerick, Ireland
Position: Prop
Height: 6'4" (1.93m)
Weight: 282lbs (128kg)
International career: 2000 - 2011
International caps: 107
International points: 10
Honours: Six Nations Triple Crown
(2004, 2006, 2007), Six Nations
Grand Slam (2009)

win over Scotland in 2005 and he was selected by Sir Clive Woodward for the subsequent Lions tour of New Zealand. He played in the warm-up against Argentina but couldn't force his way into the Test side on the tour proper.

Ireland secured Triple Crowns in 2006 and 2007, with the French denying them Grand Slams both times. Hayes was the rock at tighthead for the glorious Grand Slam of 2009, Ireland's first since 1948. Declan Kidney had revitalised the side and Hayes was still

By the age of 18 he'd developed into a man of 6'4" and nearly 19 stone. Friends convinced him to take up the sport but he initially played in the second row because of his size.

the powerhouse up front – during the championship he broke the Irish record by claiming his 94th cap. The crucial game was a one-point win over England at Croke Park but the Irish almost blew it against Wales and it needed a last-gasp drop goal from Ronan O'Gara to seal the title.

Hayes toured with the Lions again in 2009 but only played in the final Test against South Africa, by which time the series was already lost. He then became the first Irishman to earn 100 caps but he could only manage five more as he wasn't picked for the 2011 World Cup in New Zealand. He retired from all rugby at the end of the year.

Healy

A couple of caps away from joining the list of five players who have represented Ireland in 100 tests, Cian Healy is one of the top three loose head props in the world.

He began his career at Clontarf RFC where his impressive form saw him progress through the Leinster age-group system before making his senior debut in 2007.

Called up to the Irish Six Nations squad in 2008, he earned his first cap against Australia at Croke Park in 2009 - a seminal year in his career as he was involved in Leinster's Heineken Cup victory over Leicester Tigers – while he was named man-of-the-match against Australia in the 2011 World Cup, a team he clearly liked playing against.

In 2013 he was selected to tour with the British and Irish Lions, but his tour was devastatingly cut short, due to an ankle injury sustained in only the second match of the tour against the Western Force. Despite being injured for much of the 2014/15 season, Healy passed a late fitness test to be named in the 31-man Ireland squad for the 2015 Rugby World Cup.

In February 2016, Healy signed a 3-year contract extension with Leinster. He unfortunately missed the summer tour to South Africa with Ireland due to injury. A career high-light was him coming on for the last 20 minutes of the momentous victory against New Zealand in Chicago.

He was a key member of the 2018

Name: Cian Healy
Born: 7th October 1987
Dublin, Ireland
Position: Prop
Height: 6'1" (1.85m)
Weight: 258lbs (117kg)
International career: 2009 – present
International caps: 98
Honours: Six Nations Grand Slam (2018), Six Nations Championship (2014, 2015, 2018)

OPPOSITE John Hayes became the first Irishman to earn 100 caps

HEALY

Grand Slam winning team starting four of the five games including the decider against England at Twickenham on St. Patrick's Day.

In May 2019, he signed a new deal with the IRFU & Leinster until the end of the 2020/21 season having played more than 200 games for the club amassing well in excess of 100 points.

A couple of caps away from joining the list of five players who have represented Ireland in 100 tests, Cian Healy is one of the top three loose head props in the world.

Heaslip

Jamie Heaslip's father, co-founder of Ireland's elite Army Ranger Wing, was serving in Israel when Jamie was born. He returned to Kildare and attended Newbridge College, and was then selected for the national Under-21 side for the World Cup. Ireland made it to the final but were beaten by New Zealand, after which Heaslip was nominated for the Young Player of the Year award.

He joined Leinster in 2005 and was called up to the national team for the 2006 autumn internationals. By taking the field against a combined Pacific Islands team in the last match of the year, he became the 1000th player to pull on the Irish jersey. The 2007 Six Nations saw Ireland continue their fine form – as well as

beating the islanders, they'd also turned over Australia and South Africa the previous autumn – and they upset Wales in Cardiff in their opening match of the championship. They then conceded a try in the last minute against France at Croke Park and their hopes of a Grand Slam were dashed.

Ireland recovered quickly and demolished a lacklustre England the following week, and they edged past Scotland by a point in Edinburgh. England's victory over France meant that no side could achieve a Grand Slam so Ireland needed to beat Italy by 32 points on the last day to claim the title instead of France. They won 51-24 so the French secured the championship on points difference.

Eddie O'Sullivan didn't pick Heaslip for the 2007 World Cup and Ireland missed his presence and power in both the set-piece and loose and they were eliminated at the group stage. He returned to the squad for the 2008 Six Nations with only three caps under his belt but the World Cup debacle had left the team short on confidence and they only squeezed past Italy and Scotland.

If he had been something of a peripheral player so far, Heaslip con-firmed his status as a player of real talent in 2009. He scored the opening try in a tough 30-21 win over France in the first match of the Six Nations, and Ireland then demolished Italy in their second game. England ran them close at Croke Park but Ireland held on and Heaslip scored his second try of the tournament against Scotland in week four. Wales were moments away from denying the Irish a first Grand Slam in more than 60 years but O'Gara slotted a drop goal in the dying moments to send a nation into raptures. Heaslip then started in all three Tests for the

Name: James Peter Richard Heaslip
Born: 15th December 1983, Tiberias, Israel
Position: Number 8
Height: 6'4" (1.93m)
Weight: 243lbs (110kg)
International career: 2006 - 2017
International caps: 100
International points: 65
Honours: Six Nations Triple Crown (2007), Six Nations Grand Slam (2009), Lions Tour Winner (2013), Six Nations Championship (2009, 2014, 2015)

Lions in South Africa, although the hosts shaded a tight series.

It needed a last-gasp try from Brian O'Driscoll to secure a draw with Australia in that year's autumn internationals, but Ireland went on to beat Fiji and South Africa. Heaslip scored again in the first match of the 2010 Six Nations but the side suffered a surprise defeat to Scotland and finished second in the table behind France. He was then sent off against New Zealand for striking Richie McCaw on Ireland's summer tour.

He scored against France in the 2011 Six Nations but a narrow defeat left Ireland in mid-table before the World Cup. Heaslip was ever-present in the side that won all four pool games and topped their group but Wales were too strong in the quarter-final.

He couldn't add to his try tally in 2012 and Ireland then slumped to fifth place in the 2013 Six Nations with only a single win. As Heaslip was now captain, he shouldered some of the blame but he answered his critics in style on the successful Lions tour of Australia in 2013 and in the subsequent Six Nations. He scored another try in a big win over Scotland but then relinquished the captaincy to Paul O'Connell. A narrow defeat to England robbed Ireland of a second Grand Slam in five years but Ireland still won the 2014 championship.

They kicked off the 2015 Six Nations with three consecutive wins, although Heaslip missed the brutal battle against England in Dublin. A narrow loss to Wales denied them the Grand Slam but they could still secure the championship with a big win over Scotland on the last day. Although they were winning comfortably, Heaslip ensured the title stayed with Ireland when he dislodged the ball while tackling Stuart Hogg. The hit prevented a certain Scottish try that would have given England the title on points difference.

Heaslip earned 95 caps for Ireland, making him one of the country's most capped players, and possibly could have made the ton had not a seemingly innocuous injury in the warm-up against England in the 2017 Six Nations prematurely ended his career. He had however already won the World Rugby Try of the Year against Italy in the 2016 Six Nations' Championship.

Hickie

BELOW Denis Hickie at the 2007 RWC

Denis Hickie was a schoolboy player with great flat speed and quick feet, and he led St Mary's College to glory in the 1994 Leinster Schools Senior Cup. He was accepted to University College Dublin on a dual rugby/athletics scholarship and he joined Leinster in 1996. He was called up to the national team for the 1997 Five Nations and made his debut against Wales. Ireland had been soundly beaten by France the week before but a Hickie try and solid kicking from Eric Elwood restored Irish pride.

It was a short-lived resurgence, however: Hickie scored again against Scotland but Ireland lost by 28 points after already shipping 46 against England. The transition to professional rugby was blamed and, despite Hickie scoring another three tries in the following campaign, Ireland were whitewashed and collected the infamous wooden spoon.

Warren Gatland's side could only manage one win over a lacklustre Wales in the 1999 Five Nations and Hickie failed to make the squad for the

World Cup later in the year. Ireland lost to Argentina in a quarter-final playoff but Gatland began to engineer a turnaround in fortunes during the 2000 Six Nations. Progress continued in 2001 with a win over France and another against Wales – in which Hickie scored a late try under the posts – and then a surprise win over England in Dublin that spoiled the visitors' chance of a Grand Slam.

He missed out on selection for the 2001 Lions but showed the side what they'd missed with a superb display against Wales in the opening game to the 2002 Six Nations. He scored a try in the 54-10 demolition and another in a 15-point win over Italy, but Ireland could only finish third. He scored in Ireland's opener against Scotland in 2003 but they lost the Grand Slam decider to England by 40 points. He then ruptured an Achilles tendon during the World Cup.

He missed out a Triple Crown in 2004 as he continued his recovery but he roared back with two tries in the 2005 Six Nations and was selected for the subsequent Lions tour to New Zealand. He didn't make the Test team but helped the midweek side to seven wins over their provincial opposition. He also didn't make Eddie O'Sullivan's side for the 2006 Six Nations because of a dislocated fibula.

He bounced back to form with Leinster and ran the length of the field to score against Toulouse. He was recalled to the national team for the autumn internationals and scored another memorable try against Australia. He helped Ireland to another Triple Crown in 2007 and also scored a brace against Italy. He retired after a disappointing World Cup that saw Ireland eliminated at the group stage.

Name: Denis Anthony Hickie
Born: 13th February 1976, Dublin, Ireland
Position: Wing
Height: 6'2" (1.88m)
Weight: 205lbs (93kg)
International career: 1997 - 2007
International caps: 62
International points: 145
Honours: Six Nations Triple Crown (2006, 2007)

Horgan

Shane Horgan was born in Bellewstown and first played for Boyne RFC. He went to St Mary's School in Drogheda and represented Meath at Gaelic Football. Having chosen rugby, he joined Lansdowne when he left school and Leinster in 1998. The side eventually produced one of the world's greatest three-quarter divisions with Brian O'Driscoll, Gordon D'Arcy, Denis Hickie, Rob Kearney, Jonny Sexton and legendary Argentinean import Felipe Contepomi.

Playing in such illustrious company allowed Horgan's game to progress quickly and he made his debut for the national side in 2000 against Scotland. Ireland had been in the international wilderness since the switch to professionalism in 1995 but by 2000 the side was showing signs of shedding its old ways and embracing the new. England hammered them 50-18 on the first weekend of the inaugural Six Nations (Italy having been accepted into the championship) but Ireland ran in five tries the following weekend in a big win over Scotland. Horgan backed up his debut try with a brace against Italy two weeks later and another solo effort in a narrow defeat to Wales on the last weekend of the championship.

He scored two more tries in the 2001 Six Nations and was in the side that denied the English a Grand Slam in Dublin. Despite several good personal performances and Ireland finishing second in the table to England, Horgan was a surprise omission for the subsequent Lions tour to Australia. More tries followed in 2002 but Ireland were inconsistent and suffered big Six Nations defeats to England and France.

Their Grand Slam showdown with England in 2003 was something of an anti-climax as England were too strong in every department, but Horgan was more prominent at the World Cup and scored in Ireland's group wins over Romania and Namibia. A narrow defeat to Australia in the final pool match saw them pitted

against a rampant French team in the quarters and Ireland were eliminated.

Ireland were solid if not spectacular in 2004 and 2005 but Horgan was still selected for the Lions tour of New Zealand. He made three appearances from the bench but all the Tests were lost convincingly. He was tipped to make a big impact in the 2006 Six Nations but Ireland lost to France in their second game. Pride could only be restored with wins over Wales and England, and Horgan became a national hero when he scored in both matches. His second try against England at Twickenham was referred to the video referee but he hadn't put a foot in touch and the points secured the Triple Crown in the last minute of the match. The winning score also ensured he'd never have to buy a pint of Guinness for the rest of his life.

He enhanced his reputation with another spectacular try against England at Croke Park the following year but Ireland were denied a Grand Slam after a three-point loss to France. They still won the Triple Crown after a one-point victory over Scotland and finished with a flourish after a Horgan-inspired 51-24 win over Italy in Rome. He scored the odd try over the next couple of seasons but he didn't play in the historic Grand Slam of 2009 and the autumn series proved to be his swansong. He finished his international career with a try against Fiji in a 41-6 win. He tried to return for the 2011 World Cup but a long-term knee injury forced him to retire from all rugby.

Name: Shane Patrick Horgan
Born: 18th July 1978, County Meath, Ireland
Position: Wing
Height: 6'4" (1.93m)
Weight: 230lbs (105kg)
International career: 2000 - 2009
International caps: 67
International points: 105
Honours: Six Nations Triple Crown (2004, 2006, 2007)

Humphreys

David Humphreys studied at Ballymena Academy and led the school side to the 1992 Triple Crown. He was accepted by Oxford University to study law and played in the annual varsity match against Cambridge in 1995. He scored all 19 of Oxford's points – which included the full house of try, conversion, drop goal and penalty – but they lost by two.

Having left university, he signed with London Irish for three seasons but he then joined Ulster. Head coach Murray Kidd saw enough in his kicking, distribution, line breaks and tackling to select him for the national team in 1996. All fly-halves needed to kick the goals but Humphreys was also one of the game's greatest exponents of the drop goal and he repeatedly came to Ireland's rescue with difficult kicks.

This was a lean period for Irish rugby, however. They weren't the only side to get steamrolled by Jonah

Lomu's New Zealand at the 1995 World Cup but they were slow adapting to the professional era and could only beat a Welsh side that was also suffering from a lack of strength in depth during the 1996 Five Nations.

Eric Elwood assumed most of the kicking duties for the 1997 campaign but Humphreys converted Denis Hickie's try against Scotland and also added a penalty. He was the first-choice standoff for the opening match of the 1998 Five Nations but he was dropped after a one-point loss to Scotland at Lansdowne Road.

His three penalties almost gave Ireland an unexpected win over the French in 1999, and he chipped in with 19 points in a winning cause against Wales in week two. It was Ireland's only victory in the championship, however, and, despite scoring another 27 points against England and Scotland, Ireland ended up propping up the table. Between 1996 and 1999, the side only won three Five Nations matches, but their fortunes were about to change.

He scored 28 points in the 2000 championship and helped Ireland to wins over Scotland, Italy and France, but he was now competing with Ronan O'Gara for the number 10 shirt and the pair shared kicking duties for the next three seasons and at the 2003 World Cup. Humphreys contributed 18 points against Romania and another five in a one-point win over Argentina but Ireland lost to Australia in the final group game and France blew them away in the first half of the quarter-final.

Humphreys was dropped to the bench for the following Six Nations so he missed out on Ireland's Triple Crown, but he returned to captain the side while O'Gara was on duty with the Lions in 2005. He warmed the bench again for the glorious 2006 season, in which Ireland secured another Triple Crown, and retired as his country's most-capped outside-half after the championship.

He retired from domestic duty in 2008 but remained with Ulster in a coaching role for the next six years. He was then hired by Gloucester as the team's director of rugby.

Name: David Humphreys, MBE
Born: 10th September 1971, Belfast, Northern Ireland
Position: Fly-half
Height: 5'10" (1.78m)
Weight: 183lbs (83kg)
International career: 1996 - 2006
International caps: 72
International points: 560
Honours: Six Nations Triple Crown (2004, 2006)

Keane

RIGHT Moss Keane - front cover of the memoirs of " one of the most loved Irish internationals "

One of the great gentlemen of Irish Sport, Moss Keane first made a name for himself playing Gaelic football at college level and winning three Sigerson Cups, a county championship, a Munster club championship and playing in an All Ireland Club Final.

He was introduced to rugby by a friend at college and asked what he first thought about the game replied: " It was like watching a pornographic movie – very frustrating for those watching and only enjoyable for those participating! "

He made an immediate impact at lock forward, turning out for the Lansdowne Club, and earned his first international call up for Ireland in January 1974 against France in Paris. The giant Kerryman would go on to win a further 50 caps for his country. He scored his one and only test try in a victory over Scotland in 1980 and it was also against Scotland that he played his final international in Dublin, which Ireland lost heavily.

He was a key player in Ireland's 1982

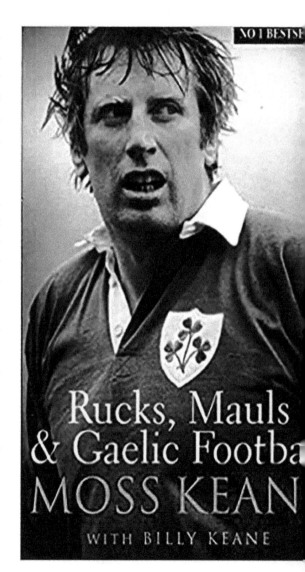

Five Nations Championships win and their historic triple crown victory but perhaps his finest moment was touring with Phil Bennett's British and Irish Lions in 1977 making one Test appearance.

He died of bowel cancer in October 2010 aged just 62 and was described by the IRFU as one of Irish rugby's " most genuine characters and legends of the game.

" Moss had the ability on the field that no one could doubt from his record at club, provincial and international elevel, " said IRFU President Caleb Powell.

In the final few lines of his autobiography, 'Rucks, Mauls And Gaelic Football', Keane reflected, in his own inimitable way, on how he would like to be remembered.

"I'm not one that thinks of how I'd like to be remembered or shite like that. I've had many great days and I've been lucky in life," he acknowledged.

"I played rugby 51 times for Ireland and made lasting friendships out of the game. What I achieved was certainly against the odds but sport can throw these things up – that's the beauty of it.

"I'd like to think that success never went to my head and that if someone, somewhere was asked, they might say, 'Moss Keane? Ah sure, he did his best.' He did his best. That would do me nicely."

Ollie Campbell (who wrote the foreword for this book), a long-standing teammate of Keane's, said: "Moss enriched every one's life that he came into contact with these past 62 years. Rugby people don't just have the Moss Keane story they have Moss Keane stories. There are many and they are all humorous. He just had a way about him — he was a one off. Certainly, he was one of the most loved Irish internationals.

"Never dropped in 11 seasons, Moss used to say that he saw off a lot of second row partners. Even if he had a bad game it was always his partner that got dropped but the longevity of his career was a tribute to his durability. "

Name: Maurice Ignatius "Moss" Keane
Born: 27th July 1948 County Kerry
Died: 5th October 2010
Position: Lock
International career: 1974-1984
International caps: 52
International points: 4
Honours: Five Nations Championship (1974, 1982) Five Nations Triple Crown 1982

Kearney

Rob Kearney began his sporting career as an athlete and Gaelic footballer and he made the Cooley youth team for the Louth Senior Football Championship final in 2004. (His brother David was also a standout player who would later join him at Leinster.) Kearney went to Clongowes Wood College before heading to Dublin University. He helped the university's Under-20 rugby side to the McCorry Cup before joining Leinster at the age of 19 in 2005.

Having represented the club as a schoolboy and at Under-19 level, Kearney was chosen for the senior team for a friendly against Parma. He scored a hat-trick on debut and was drafted into the squad for the Celtic League game against Neath-Swansea Ospreys. Leinster won by two points but he would taste defeat in that season's Heineken Cup at home to Bath.

...Kearney then exploded into the international scene with a super try in a big win against Scotland.

His route into the Ireland side mirrored his ascent to greatness at club level: schoolboy and Under-19 caps led to selection for Ireland's A-team and a summer tour that included the Churchill Cup. He was also asked to join the senior squad for their training camp before the 2005 autumn international series but he didn't make the team itself until the 2008 Six Nations.

Ireland were poor in their opening match of the campaign and only just edged past Italy in Dublin but, despite a much-improved performance the following weekend, they still lost by five points to the French in Paris. Kearney then exploded into the international scene with a super try in a big win against Scotland. Wales managed to win by four at Croke Park and England were too strong at Twickenham but Kearney crossed the whitewash in the latter match to round off an impressive debut season.

Ireland finally delivered their second Grand Slam in 2009 after scintillating victories over France, England and a nail-biter against Wales that Ronan O'Gara won with virtually the last kick of the match. His domestic form was equally impressive and he scored 10 tries in 10 appearances in the build-up to Leinster's historic Heineken Cup victory in 2009. He was a shoo-in for the British Lions in South Africa later in the year and he scored the tourists' only try in a narrow defeat that also saw the hosts

Name: Robert Kearney
Born: 26th March 1986, Dundalk, Ireland
Position: Fullback / Wing
Height: 6'1" (1.85m)
Weight: 210lbs (95kg)
International career: 2008 - present
International caps: 98
International points: 87
Honours: Six Nations Grand Slam (2009, 2018), Lions Series Winner (2013), Six Nations Championship (2009, 2014, 2015, 2018)

LEFT Rob Kearney playing for Ireland at the Rugby World Cup 2015

take the series.

He was selected for the 2011 World Cup in New Zealand and bounced back from an injury against the USA in the first game to help the side to the quarter-final. He toured again with the victorious Lions in Australia in 2013 and helped Ireland to another Six Nations Championship in 2014, by which time his brother had also been drafted into the squad.

Kearney was denied a Grand Slam in 2015 after a narrow loss to Wales, but a big win over Scotland on the last day of the championship secured the Six Nations title on points difference from both England and the Welsh.

As well as playing in three World Cups and 11 Six Nations Championships, Kearney is the only Irish player who started all 20 games in the Grand Slams of 2009 and 2018, as well as the back-to-back titles of 2014 and 2015.

RIGHT Rob Kearney in full flight

Kiernan

Tom Kiernan was an exceptional player in his youth and he was tipped for greatness from an early age. He didn't disappoint and went on to become one of the game's great fullbacks. He joined Munster and was fast-tracked into the Ireland side at the age of only 21. By the time he retired in 1973 he'd racked up the most Test appearances by an Irishman (54), most Tests as captain (22), most points (158) and two tours with the Lions.

Name: Thomas Joseph Kiernan
Born: 7th January 1939, Cork, Ireland
Position: Fullback
Height: 5'10" (1.78m)
Weight: 161lbs (73kg)
International career: 1960 - 1973
International caps: 64
International points: 228
Honours: Five Nations Championship (1973)

It's unusual for a fullback to captain a side but Kiernan was so influential for Ireland that, having already toured with the Lions twice, he was chosen to lead the 1968 tourists to South Africa. He had only played once for the team before but on this trip he played in all four internationals, although the series was eventually lost 3-0, the same result as back in 1962. The midweek side enjoyed great success, however, winning 15 of their 16 matches and only losing to Transvaal.

Five years after his international retirement he coached Munster to perhaps their greatest win when they defeated the All Blacks, the first time any Irish team had beaten the Kiwis in more than a century.

BELOW Tom Kiernan

Kyle

Jack Kyle has been voted Ireland's best player, and there are some in New Zealand and Australia who rate him as the greatest Lion. The Belfast-born fly-half was lightning-quick over short distances, delivered precise passes and could step off both feet and leave defenders clutching thin air. He was also a fine kicker and a better tackler than most people gave him credit for.

BELOW Jack Kyle makes a weaving run

This combination of speed and skill helped Ireland to their first Grand Slam in 1948 but he did have the odd lapse in concentration such as against England when, with the Grand Slam beckoning, Barney Mullan's penalty bounced back off the crossbar into his hands. Kyle threw a long pass out wide but England wing Dicky Guest second-guessed the play and he made the interception before running the length of the field to score. When he added the conversion, the Irish lead was cut to a single point. Thankfully for the outside-half, the final whistle saved the Irish from a late English onslaught and his error didn't cost Ireland the Grand Slam.

On the 1950 Lions tour to New Zealand, Kyle earned both his spurs and the respect of the world's greatest players. Still only 24, he was a sufficiently rounded talent to be named in *New Zealand Rugby Almanac's* players of the year.

With the likes of Jack Matthews and Bleddyn Williams in the centre, he could always play on the gain line and his passing gave these devastating runners the time and space they needed to scythe through the All Black defence. His best game came in the first Test in which he scored a spectacular solo try having counterattacked from a miscued kick. He sliced through the Kiwi rearguard, then set up another try for Jones with a pinpoint kick, and also won the penalty that almost gave them the game. The Lions could only draw 9-9, however, and the series slipped away when they narrowly lost the next three Tests.

He scored another try in the 24-3 defeat of Australia on the second leg of the tour. He was also on hand to guide Ireland to another Five Nations Championship in 1951, although the remainder of the decade wasn't as successful. He retired from international rugby in 1958 having played 46 times for his country and six times for the Lions. Six years later he hung up his club boots and began work on a humanitarian program in Indonesia and Sumatra. He also worked as a consultant surgeon for 35 years in Zambia.

In 2001 he returned to County Down and helped fund the Bursary scheme for the Queen's University Rugby Academy. In 2008 he was inducted into the IRB Hall of Fame. He died in 2014 after a long illness.

Name: John Wilson 'Jack' Kyle, OBE
Born: 10th January 1926, Belfast, Northern Ireland
Died: 27th November 2014, Bryansford, Northern Ireland
Position: Fly-half
International career: 1946 - 1958
International caps: 52
International points: 30
Honours: Five Nations Grand Slam (1948), Five Nations Championship (1948, 1951)

LEFT Jack Kyle kicks to touch

McBride

Of all the players linked with the story of Irish rugby and the Lions, one individual stands out: Willie John McBride. This sporting titan was five times a tourist and leader of the most successful tour in the Lions' history. He is also the man who personified their famous team spirit, but it might have been so different. He was in his late teens before he considered rugby, but when he devoted his attention to the game his rise to superstardom was as quick as it was inevitable. At 21 he was an Ireland international and in 1962 he came on in the third and fourth Lions' Tests in South Africa.

The 1966 tour was less successful and the Lions were whitewashed by the All Blacks, but playing in all four Tests on the 1968 South Africa trip helped exorcise his demons and, with the emergence of the Welsh wizards, he knew the Lions had a bright future.

The lock hewn from Ballymena granite eventually played in 17 Tests for the tourists but he endured nine straight defeats before tasting victory against the All Blacks in 1971. His appointment as pack leader during the trip saw an upsurge in the side's fortunes and he was selected as captain for the subsequent tour of South Africa on the back of four big performances. Much of the same team accompanied him three years later.

The Lions had been put under pressure not to go as the country was struggling with its apartheid regime and protesters gathered at every hotel, but the incentive for the players was that no touring side, including the great New Zealanders, had ever beaten the Springboks at home.

McBride recalled another obstacle the

tourists faced: "You know you're up against it when the ref shouts 'our ball' at the put-in to the scrum."

Having voiced his concerns over the standards set by referees, as well as the blatant violence from the Springboks towards his own team, McBride introduced the most famous call in rugby history: the '99'. At the sound of the words 'ninety-nine' every Lion would stop what they were doing and belt the nearest South African player. He claimed there was method in this madness as too many of his players were being singled out for punishment. At the call there would be 30 seconds of violence and then the match would continue. The referee couldn't send all the players from the field and the South Africans couldn't keep interrupting play by scrapping. It was an unsatisfactory medium but getting their retaliation in first worked: the Lions were unbeaten throughout the 22-match tour and won the Test series.

McBride stands astride the legend of the Lions like a colossus, and to this day Willie John remains the alpha male, leader of the pride. His career with Ireland lasted another year and it took until his final match against France at Lansdowne Road before he scored his first try.

Having retired, he took over as coach of the national team and was the manager for the 1983 Lions tour to New Zealand. In 1997, he was one of the first inductees into the IRB Hall of Fame, and in 2004 he was named *Rugby World*'s personality of the century. He was awarded a CBE in the 2019 New Years' Honours list for his services to Rugby Union.

> LEFT Willie John McBride poses for a Lions pre-tour photo

Name: William James 'Willie John' McBride, MBE
Born: 6th June 1940, Antrim, Northern Ireland
Position: Lock
Height: 6'3" (1.92m)
Weight: 225lbs (102kg)
International career: 1962 - 1975
International caps: 80
International points: 7
Honours: Lions Series Winner (1971, 1974), Five Nations Championship (1973)

This sporting titan was five times a tourist and leader of the most successful tour in the Lions' history.

McKay

Bill McKay was called up to the war effort and served as a Royal Marine Commando. He made his international debut for Ireland against France at Lansdowne Road in the third Five Nations match after the war. The visitors won by four points but McKay was the standout flanker on both sides and

RIGHT Bill McKay (far left) joins his team at Dublin Station before the 1951 Five Nations match against England. Jack Kyle is third from left

he helped the Irish demolish England 22-0 in Dublin in the second round of matches. Ireland narrowly beat Scotland and lost to Wales in Swansea to finish mid-table but the following season was to be their annus mirabilis.

Ireland swept all before them and secured their first Grand Slam, although the English almost spoiled the party when Jack Kyle threw a telegraphed pass that Dicky Guest intercepted. Thankfully it didn't affect the result and McKay was selected for the British Lions after another championship-winning season in 1949 (the French won in Dublin to

---

Name: James William 'Bill' McKay
Born: 12th July 1921, Waterford, Ireland
Died: 15th October 1997, Gisborne, New Zealand
Position: Flanker
International career: 1947 - 1952
International caps: 29
International points: 9
Honours: Five Nations Grand Slam (1948), Five Nations Championship (1948, 1949, 1951), Lions Series Winner (1950)

---

deny them back-to-back Grand Slams).

Having racked up 17 consecutive internationals, McKay, along with tour captain Karl Mullen, was the most experienced forward to travel to Australia and New Zealand in 1950. He was the standout player on the tour and scored more tries than any other forward (10 in 15 starts for the midweek and Test sides), the first of which came on debut against Buller. He then scored a brace against both Auckland and New South Wales Country.

Having impressed the selectors with his ball-handling skills in the loose as well as his tackling and running, he was picked for all six Tests against the All Blacks and the Wallabies. The Lions played a high-tempo attacking style of rugby that won them praise and respect from the locals.

McKay put in a man-of-the-match performance in the first Test in New Zealand, but he broke his nose and picked up a concussion midway through the second Test so he couldn't play in any of the provincial games leading into the third Test. (During his recovery, McKay was looked after by former New Zealand international Maurice Brownlie at home in Gisborne.) Such was McKay's

influence that he was picked again for the decisive match.

The All Blacks won the series 3-0 after narrow victories in final three internationals but McKay's tour ended on a positive note when the Lions won both Tests against Australia on their way home. His contribution to the tour was incalculable and many thought him the best player in all six Tests.

Having returned home, he helped Ireland to another Five Nations Championship in 1951 (a 3-3 draw with Wales denied them a Grand Slam). He then qualified as a doctor at Queen's University Belfast before emigrating to Gisborne in New Zealand, an area that he had fallen in love with while touring the land of the long white cloud with the Lions.

Millar

Not even the great Willie John McBride can match Syd Millar's Lions' record. He has been part of the side in some capacity for nearly half a century, playing on three tours, managing the team in South Africa in 1980, acting as chairman on the 2001 tour to Australia, selector in 1977, 1993 and 1997, and as an active member on the rugby board that oversaw the 2013 Lions on their victorious Australian tour.

The Ballymena and Ireland prop started playing at standoff half but he grew too big for the position. Thankfully, he retained his ball skills and he was always a dangerous force in the loose. He first played for his country in 1958 and he toured with the Lions in 1959 and 1962. He was extremely versatile and could play on either side of the scrum, and he eventually played in 16 of the tourists' 24 matches on the latter tour. He was then, somewhat surprisingly, dropped by Ireland and had to wait another

He first played for his country in 1958 and he toured with the Lions in 1959 and 1962. He was extremely versatile and could play on either side of the scrum.

three years before winning the final 14 of his 37 caps and gaining selection for his third tour as a Lions player. He finally retired from international rugby in 1970.

He visited South Africa again and returned as part of the coaching staff on the all-conquering 1974 tour, with Alun Thomas the standout member of his team. The 1980 trip presented a very different challenge given that the country was in the grip of apartheid and the Lions came under close scrutiny for their attitude to the policy. Millar dealt with the issue superbly and allowed the team to do its talking on the pitch.

Millar rated the 1959 side as the best he ever played in, but the 1974 tour will be remembered as his finest hour with the Lions.

Name: John Sydney 'Syd' Millar, CBE
Born: 23rd May 1934, Ballymena, Ireland
Position: Prop
Height: 6'0" (1.83m)
Weight: 224lbs (102kg)
International career: 1958 - 1970
International caps: 46
International points: 0
Honours: Three Lions Tours (1959 - 1968), Lions Tour Coach (1974)

The Ballymena and Ireland prop started playing at standoff half but he grew too big for the position. Thankfully, he retained his ball skills and he was always a dangerous force in the loose.

Miller

Eric Miller was a multi-talented athlete who played rugby, cricket and Gaelic Football while at Wesley College in Dublin. He also played football for Leicester Celtic alongside Damian Duff. In 1995, he finally chose to concentrate on rugby and joined Old Wesley and, later that year, he was selected for Leinster.

The following year he joined Leicester Tigers in the top flight of English rugby and made such an impact in the Heineken Cup that he was called up to the national side. He'd already represented his country at schoolboy and Under-21 level (with whom he won a Triple Crown in 1996), but his debut for the senior team came against Italy in a friendly before the 1997 Five Nations. He made such an impact in his first campaign that he was asked to tour South Africa with the Lions in the summer. Despite being the youngest member of the party at only 21, he started five matches against the provinces and would have made the first Test had he not gone down with flu.

He started the second Test on June 28th when the Lions made history and clinched the series. He missed the third Test with an injury but continued his incredible form in the 1998 and 1999 Five Nations, although Ireland were still coming to terms with the professional era and only won one match.

Ireland may have lost heavily to Australia in the pool stage of the 1999

LEFT Eric Miller played for Leinster and Ireland for nearly a decade

MILLER

Name: Eric Roger Patrick Miller
Born: 23rd September 1975, Dublin, Ireland
Position: Number 8
Height: 6'3" (1.91m)
Weight: 238lbs (108kg)
International career: 1997 - 2005
International caps: 49
International points: 30
Honours: Lions Series Winner (1997), Six Nations Triple Crown (2004)

World Cup but they were still expected to see off Argentina in a quarter-final playoff in Lens. The South Americans surprised the men in green, however, and Ireland were eliminated.

The new millennium brought an upsurge in fortunes and, under Warren Gatland, Ireland won three matches in the Five Nations. Despite unexpectedly losing to Scotland in the 2001 Five Nations, Miller's Ireland dashed England's Grand Slam hopes with a 20-14 win at Lansdowne Road in October. When Eddie O'Sullivan took over as coach, Ireland continued to improve and won another three matches in 2002. They lost a Grand Slam decider against England the following year but Miller was ever-present in the side that performed well at the 2003 World Cup in Australia. He scored a brace against Namibia, although Ireland eventually bowed at the quarter-final stage after a heavy defeat to France.

Miller played his last international against Japan in 2005. Having retired from top-flight rugby, he pursued a brief Gaelic Football career. Since 2016 he has held various coaching positions including latterly the men's senior first team in Arklow Rugby Club as well as Catholic University School in Dublin.

Mullen

Name: Karl Daniel Mullen
Born: 26th November 1926, Courtown Harbour, Ireland
Died: 26th April 2009, Kilcullen
Position: Hooker
International career: 1947 - 1952
International caps: 28
International points: 0
Honours: Five Nations Grand Slam (1948), Five Nations Championship (1948, 1949, 1951), Lions Series Winner (1950)

Educated at Belvedere College and the Royal College of Surgeons, Karl Mullen played for Old Belvedere RFC and he was immediately tipped as a future captain of his country. He earned the first of his 25 Ireland caps as a hooker against France in the 1947 Five Nations campaign, although he had previously played in uncapped games against France, England, Wales and Scotland in 1946.

Mullen took over his country's captaincy during the 1948 Five Nations Championship and, with his laidback but determined style of play, he guided the side to a famous Triple Crown and then to a historic first Grand Slam (he and the seven surviving members of that team witnessed Ireland's next Grand Slam in the 2009 Six Nations Championship).

He led the same side to a second Triple Crown in 1949 and was promptly selected as British & Irish Lions captain for the upcoming tour to Australia and New Zealand. He eventually played in 17 games on the tour, including three Test matches, of which he won one, drew one and lost one. He was injured for the final two Tests against the All Blacks and his leadership and ball skills were sorely missed. The Lions were much the weaker in his absence and lost the series.

He retired from international rugby with 25 Ireland caps after his side's 14-3 defeat to Wales at Lansdowne Road at the end of the 1952 Five Nations. He continued to play a role in the game and served as President of Leinster in 1963-64 as well as Chairman of the Irish selectors. This incomparable hooker died in 2009 after a long illness.

BELOW
Karl Mullen laces up his boots before a big game

Mulcahy

Bill Mulcahy was educated at St Munchin's College in Limerick and Dublin University. Having forged a formidable reputation as a schoolboy rugby player, he joined Leinster in 1955 and was called up to the national team (along with five other debutants: Ronnie Dawson, Dave Hewitt, James Donaldson, Noel Murphy and James Stevenson) for the visit of the touring Australians in January 1958. The scores were level at 3-3 at the end of the first half but the hosts won the game – their first ever victory over the Wallabies – with a Cecil Pedlow penalty. Ireland could only manage a single win in that year's Five Nations, however, and the glory years of Jack Kyle and Karl Mullen at the dawn of the decade suddenly seemed a long time ago.

Ireland showed marked improvement in 1959 and beat both Scotland and France on their way to second place in the table. Mulcahy was the powerhouse in the engine room and he was selected to tour Australia and New Zealand with the British & Irish Lions later in the summer. Apart from a brief loss of form in the second match against New South Wales on the first leg of the

> **Name:** William 'Bill' Albert Mulcahy
> **Born:** 7th January 1935, Limerick, Ireland
> **Position:** Lock
> **Height:** 6'1" (1.85m)
> **Weight:** 225lbs (102kg)
> **International career:** 1958 - 1965
> **International caps:** 41
> **International points:** 0
> **Honours:** Lions Series Winner (1959)

ABOVE Bill Mulcahy leaps for the Lions

tour, the Lions were unstoppable and they won both Tests against Australia comfortably. They then won all but one of their warm-up games before the four Tests against the All Blacks. Mulcahy missed the first three Tests but played in the fourth, which turned out to be the tourists' only victory.

Ireland were dismal in 1960 and couldn't win a match in the Five Nations, and they only managed a single win over England in 1961. Despite being whitewashed again in 1962, Mulcahy was a diamond in the rough and he was chosen to tour South Africa with the Lions later that summer. He played in all four Tests but the hosts were simply too strong and the Lions could only manage a draw and three defeats. He finally avenged the disappointment with Ireland in 1965 when they recorded their first-ever win (9-6) against the Springboks at Lansdowne Road. Mulcahy retired later that year as one of Ireland's greatest players, tireless in the loose and fearless in the tackle. He was inducted into the Guinness Hall of Fame in 2009.

Murphy

Geordan Murphy went to Newbridge College and the Waterford Institute of Technology but he initially showed promise at Gaelic Football and represented Kildare in the All-Ireland Football Championship in 1995. Rugby ran in the family, however (his six siblings all played to a high standard), so he signed for Leicester Tigers for the first of 316 appearances in 1997.

As he graduated through the ranks in England, he was selected for Ireland at Under-21 level, but it wasn't until 2000 that he finally broke into the senior team. The previous Five Nations campaigns had brought little rewards but Warren Gatland and Eddie O'Sullivan shook up the domestic scene in the provinces and the national team benefited immediately. Having won only three Five Nations games since the sport turned professional at the end of 1995, the new millennium saw an upsurge in Ireland's fortunes.

They won three matches in the 2000 Five Nations and Murphy was given his first cap in an 83-3 victory over the USA in June. He scored two tries and chipped in with another as Ireland crushed Japan 78-9 in the autumn series.

On the domestic front, Murphy was a key figure in Leicester's Heineken Cup wins in 2001 and 2002. Had Ireland not suffered a surprise defeat to Scotland in the 2001 Six Nations, Murphy might have helped the side to a Grand Slam but they had to make do with second in the table behind England. They lost to England in a Grand Slam decider in 2003 and Murphy then broke his leg in a warm-up match against Scotland before the World Cup.

There were rumours of a rift between him and O'Sullivan, and he also had to fight for his place with Girvan Dempsey and Rob Kearney, but Murphy was still in the squad for the glorious 2009 Grand Slam-winning campaign. Having picked up a serious ankle injury playing for Leicester, he only played a peripheral role in the 2011 World Cup and retired from international rugby after the tour-

RIGHT Geordan Murphy playing for Leicester

Murphy was given his first cap in an 83-3 victory over the USA in June. He scored two tries and chipped in with another as Ireland crushed Japan 78-9 in the autumn series.

nament. He played on with Leicester until 2013 (and is still their leading try-scorer and appearance holder in the European Cup) and then took up a coaching role with the side culminating in being appointed Head Coach in December 2018.

Name: Geordan Edward Andrew Murphy
Born: 19th April 1978, Dublin, Ireland
Position: Fullback / Wing
Height: 6'1" (1.85m)
Weight: 192lbs (87kg)
International career: 2000 - 2011
International caps: 74
International points: 98
Honours: Six Nations Grand Slam (2009)

Murray

Conor Murray was another graduate of St Munchin's College who also played for Munster Schools alongside Keith Earls. He made his debut for the province against Connacht in 2010 but took a couple of seasons to establish himself in the senior team and was initially restricted to appearances from the bench. By the 2011-12 season he'd put in man-of-the-match performances in the Heineken Cup against Northampton Saints and had also been capped by the national side in the build-up to the World Cup.

He came on as a sub against France and England and his performances saw him make the final 30-man squad for the tournament in New Zealand. Ireland stuttered in their opening match against the United States but the men in green finally exorcised the ghosts of previous defeats to Australia in another epic pool game. Two more wins against Russia and Italy saw Ireland through to a quarter-final against Wales. Murray had graduated from peripheral player to the first-choice number nine in only two months but Wales were too strong in Wellington and Ireland were eliminated after a 22-10 defeat.

Murray had shown enough promise for coach Declan Kidney to stick with him for the subsequent Six Nations campaign. Ireland suffered another narrow defeat to the Welsh in their opening match but he played an hour of their big win over Italy before being replaced by rival Eoin Reddan. Murray started in the 17-17 draw with France but, despite taking the lead, the French fought back and Reddan came on after an hour when Murray picked up a knee injury that ruled him out for the rest of the tournament.

He played in all three Tests against the All Blacks on Ireland's summer tour. Despite scoring his first international try, the Kiwis were a class apart and their 60-0 demolition of the visitors remains Ireland's heaviest defeat. The 2013 Six Nations saw little improvement and Ireland could only manage a single win against Wales. Their humiliation was complete after a 22-15 loss to Italy on the final weekend.

The side was much improved by the autumn international series and registered a big win over Samoa. A heavy defeat to Australia was soon forgotten as Ireland raced to a 22-7 lead over the All Blacks in the last international of the year. Murray, Rory Best and Rob Kearney all scored tries but the Kiwis recovered to take an epic match 24-22 with the last kick of the game. Ireland took a newfound confidence into 2014 and won the Six Nations. Only England denied them a Grand Slam.

Ireland maintained this form in the autumn series by beating South Africa and Australia, and they made a solid start to the 2015 Six Nations with three consecutive wins. Murray was denied another shot at a Grand Slam after a narrow loss to Wales in their fourth match, but a big win over Scotland on the last day of the championship secured the title on points difference.

Over the past five years, Murray has been a colossus for Munster and Ireland, starting every game for his country as they won a Grand Slam in the 2018 Six Nations Championship. He also had a starring role in the Lions' drawn series against the All Blacks in 2017 – scoring a try in the second test victory and making him the first northern hemisphere player to score four tries against New Zealand.

Name: Conor Murray
Born: 20th April 1989, Limerick, Ireland
Position: Scrum-half
Height: 6'2" (1.88m)
Weight: 209lbs (95kg)
International career: 2011 - present
International caps: 86
International points: 92
Honours: Lions Series Winner (2013), Six Nations Grand Slam (2018), Six Nations Championship (2014, 2015, 2018)

BELOW Conor Murray playing for Ireland at the Rugby World Cup 2015

O'Brien

Every known accolade has been used to describe Sean O'Brien but in his prime he was arguably the most destructive open field runner in the Northern Hemisphere.

A dangerous, aggressive flanker or powerful ball-carrying No.8, he made an immediate impact on the openside and won recognition with Ireland 'A' and the full Test side at the end of 2009.

In November 2010 he made a first Test start against Samoa at Lansdowne Road, but it was his Heineken Cup form for his province later that season that sounded alarm bells that a major talent was emerging.

Scoring four tries in Leinster's six Pool games, he also ably deputised for Jamie Heaslip - and not just at provincial level because he was entrusted with the Ireland No.8 jersey for the Six Nations opener against Italy in Rome in February 2011.

Heaslip returned for the following week's encounter with France but O'Brien's services were retained by head coach Declan Kidney, who switched the versatile Carlow native to blindside flanker, thus underlining his growing importance to the current Ireland side.

And O'Brien found himself in the 30-man squad for the World Cup despite being injured going into the warm-up Tests. O'Brien played in all six of Ireland's games in the global gathering as they were knocked out at the quarter-final stage of the tournament. He went on to play in four of Ireland's five matches in

Name: Sean Kevin O'Brien
Born: 14th February 1987
Carlow, Ireland
Position: Flanker, Number 8
Height: 6"2" (1.88m)
Weight: 238lbs (108kg)
International career: 2009-2019
International caps: 61
International points: 35
Honours:

the 2012 Six Nations.

O'Brien continued his strong form into the following season and after being one of Ireland's better players during the 2013 Six Nations, he was selected for the British & Irish Lions squad in both 2013 (when he was involved from the start of the crucial third test which the Lions won to secure a first tour victory since 2001) and 2017 making five appearances and scoring five points.

Not a stranger to controversy, O'Brien punched Pascal Pape in the first minute of a win over France in the final pool match of the 2015 Rugby World Cup. He was cited by World Rugby and received a one-game ban meaning he was unable to play in the quarter final which Ireland lost to Argentina.

A fiercely protective player it was fitting that he joined London Irish in 2019 where the club's mascot is an Irish Wolfhound!

O'Callaghan

An abrasive and courageous lock, Donnchadh O'Callaghan almost racked up a century of caps for his country and he was renowned for his big hits in the loose and tireless graft. He represented Ireland at various junior levels and helped the side to the World Youth Championship in 1998 alongside future Ireland and Lions' captain Brian O'Driscoll, as well as Paddy Wallace.

He made his international debut against Wales in a tight game at the Millennium Stadium in 2003 but he then struggled to hold down a place until selected by Clive Woodward for the 2005 Lions in New Zealand. The tour may not have been a great success but his partnership in the engine room with Paul O'Connell was one of the highlights and the pairing soon became a permanent fixture in the green of Ireland, as well as with Munster on the domestic front. He had a fabulous 2009 when he won the Grand Slam with Ireland and the

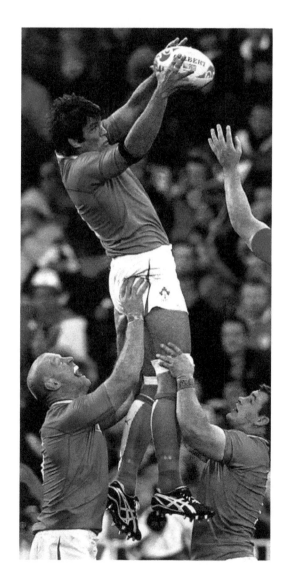

RIGHT Donnchadh O'Callaghan wins the lineout ball

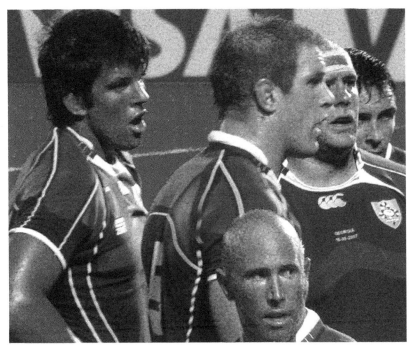

Ireland vs Georgia, 2007 Rugby World Cup, O'Callaghan on the far left

Name: Donnchadh Fintan O'Callaghan
Born: 24th March 1979, Cork, Ireland
Position: Lock
Height: 6'6" (1.98m)
Weight: 257lbs (116kg)
International career: 2003 - 2013
International caps: 98
International points: 5
Honours: Six Nations Grand Slam (2009) Six Nations Triple Crown (2004, 2006, 2007, 2009)

Magners League with Munster, having also won Heineken Cups in 2006 and 2008.

The year was capped with selection for the 2009 Lions tour to South Africa and he had the honour of captaining the side against the Southern Kings, which ended with the tourists winning comfortably, 20-8. He came on as a replacement for Alun Wyn-Jones in the first Test in Durban but couldn't help the Lions salvage a late win. He was not included in the squads for the next two Tests.

He was ever-present for Ireland throughout 2009 and 2010, and he started every game at the 2011 World Cup. He earned his 90th cap against Argentina in 2012 and was included in the 2013 Six Nations squad but he retired after the tournament.

He has been an ambassador for UNICEF since 2009.

O'Connell

Paul O'Connell was a superb swimmer and rugby player at school. He played at youth levels for his country and represented the Irish Schools in 1998 alongside future international team-mate Gordon d'Arcy. He then joined long-time second-row partner Donncha O'Callaghan in the national Under-21 squad before finally being selected for the senior side for a match against Wales in the 2002 Six Nations. He scored a try on debut – although he remembered little about it as he'd been concussed after headbutting Craig Quinnell's elbow – and was selected for the Rugby World Cup in 2003.

Ireland comfortably beat Romania and Namibia in their opening games but they only squeezed past Argentina by a single point in their third match. The final group game was another classic against hosts Australia but this time it was the Wallabies who won by a point. This narrow defeat set up a quarter-final with France but, despite scoring three converted tries, Ireland were comprehensively outplayed and lost 43 – 21.

The following year O'Connell stood in for the injured Brian O'Driscoll as captain of the national team. When Sir Clive Woodward needed a towering presence in the pack to compete with Ali Williams, Brad Thorne and Chris Jack on the 2005 Lions tour to New Zealand, the giant Munster-man was the obvious candidate. He played in every Test but the Lions couldn't compete with a dominant All Black pack and they were whitewashed in the series.

He then helped Ireland to the Triple Crown and was the only northern hemisphere nominee for the world player of the year. He captained the side once more in their historic demolition of England at Croke Park (43-13) in 2007, then captained club side Munster to European Cup glory. The World Cup later that year was a huge disappointment: Ireland only just overcame minnows Namibia and Georgia but were beaten by Argentina and France and crashed out of the tournament at the group stage.

O'Connell recovered his form and was again the standout lock on the 2009 Lions tour to South Africa, a role which saw him earn the captaincy and almost secure the series. He also oversaw Ireland's first Grand Slam in 61 years. He led the side at the 2011 World Cup, which included another epic match against Australia (Ireland won 15-6), but the Irish could only reach the quarter-final.

He recovered from several serious knee injuries in early 2013 and was selected for the Lions tour to Australia later that year. He fractured an arm in the thrilling first Test victory but remained with the squad to help guide them to their first series win since 1997. O'Connell was back to his best in the 2014 autumn internationals as Ireland beat South Africa and Australia.

He then led the side to the Six Nations title in 2015. The Welsh denied him another Grand Slam but a try in a big win over Scotland on the last day secured the championship on points difference from England and Wales.

He bowed out from international rugby as captain of his country at the 2015 Rugby World Cup where a bad hamstring injury in Ireland's win against France ruled him out of the tournament and forced him to retire from professional rugby and his new club Toulon without playing a match. He now works for BBC Sport as a pundit and commentator.

Name: Paul Jeremiah O'Connell
Born: 20th October 1979, Limerick, Ireland
Position: Lock
Height: 6'6" (1.98m)
Weight: 242lbs (110kg)
International career: 2002- 2015
International caps: 115
International points: 40
Honours: Six Nations Triple Crown (2004, 2006, 2007, 2009), Six Nations Grand Slam (2009), Six Nations Championship (2009, 2014, 2015), Lions Series Winner (2013)

O'Driscoll

Brian O'Driscoll was one of the most feared centres in world rugby. Blessed with great strength, a brutal hand-off, devastating side-step, good flat speed and a bone-shaking tackle, he was one of the few players who would walk into any side in the game.

He was born in Dublin and initially gravitated to Gaelic Football but a spell at Blackrock College convinced him to pursue rugby and he made the senior cup team in 1996, a year in which he was also capped by Ireland Schools. He joined Leinster in 1999 and helped the side to the semi-final of the 2003 European Cup.

His good early form for the club's Second XV saw him selected for Ireland in a humbling 46-10 defeat to Australia. In 2000, he lit up the international stage with a hat-trick against France in Paris, and, the following year, he had his personal revenge over Australia when he

Blessed with great strength, a brutal hand-off, devastating sidestep, good flat speed and a bone-shaking tackle, he was one of the few players who would walk into any side in the game.

scored a fabulous individual try for the Lions at the Gabba that secured the tourists the first Test. They couldn't take the series, however, but he did then guide Ireland to a first win over the Wallabies since 1979.

More success with club and country followed and he was the standout candidate as captain for the 2005 Lions tour to New Zealand. His tour ended just two minutes into the first Test, however, when he was spear tackled by Tana Umaga and Keven Mealamu, aggravating an old shoulder injury. It was a sad end to what could have been a terrific series for the Irishman, although it's doubtful whether his presence alone would have been enough to see off a strong All Black side.

He was back to his blistering and combative best in the first Test of the 2009 series against South Africa when he provided two assists, but the Lions ran out of steam and went down 26-21. He was concussed in the second match

Name: Brian Gerald O'Driscoll
Born: 21st January 1979, Dublin, Ireland
Position: Centre
Height: 5'10" (1.78m)
Weight: 205lbs (93kg)
International career: 1999 - 2014
International caps: 141
International points: 250
Honours: Six Nations Triple Crown (2004, 2006, 2007), Six Nations Grand Slam (2009), Lions Series Winner (2013), Six Nations Championship (2009, 2014)

He had his personal revenge over Australia when he scored a fabulous individual try for the Lions at the Gabba.

O'DRISCOLL

and missed the third Test. With 141 international caps, 47 tries and 250 points in the bank, O'Driscoll is one of the modern game's true greats, and Will Carling placed him in the top 10 of all time.

His record at the Rugby World Cup was mixed, however. He scored two tries in the pool matches in 1999 but Ireland blew up in their playoff against Argentina and failed to make the quarter-finals. In 2003, O'Driscoll was his side's go-to man but, despite scoring a try and a drop-goal, Ireland came up short against hosts Australia in the group, and they were then thumped 43-21 by France in the knockout phase. The Irish underperformed in 2007 but topped their qualifying group in 2011 with a memorable revenge win over Australia. They then ran into an inspired Wales and again failed to make it past the quarter-final stage.

O'Driscoll was back to his best in the first game of the 2013 Six Nations and was selected to tour with the Lions in Australia later that year. He played the first two Tests of the series but looked a little below par and Warren Gatland controversially dropped him for the deciding Test in Sydney. The coach's decision was

vindicated, however, as the Lions ran out comfortable victors (41-16).

O'Driscoll enjoyed a fabulous swansong to his international career when he scored a hat-trick against Italy in the 2014 Six Nations and then guided Ireland to the title with a rare victory over France in Paris.

He was inducted into the World Rugby Hall of Fame in November 2016.

LEFT Brian O'Driscoll on a trademark powerful run

ABOVE Brian O'Driscoll is honoured before his final Test match in 2014

O'Gara

Although Ronan O'Gara was born in the USA, his family moved back to Ireland and he went to college and university in Cork. He played rugby for both but joined Munster in 1997 and was called up to the national side against Scotland in 2000 at the age of 23. For most of the next decade, he and Ulster fly-half David Humphreys competed for the same jersey, and they would eventually play in 200 internationals between them, although O'Gara enjoyed the lion's share.

He toured Australia with the Lions in 2001 and may have pushed Jonny Wilkinson for a place in the Test series but for a fight with New South Wales opposite number Duncan McRae that left O'Gara with a terrible facial wound. Two years later, he cemented his place in the side during a Six Nations campaign that saw Ireland and England fighting for a Grand Slam in the final match. England may have won the title but Ireland were confident going into the 2003 World Cup. They qualified from a tough group

but lost to the French in the quarter-final.

In 2004, Ireland lost their first match of the Six Nations to the French but they bounced back to win their first Triple Crown since 1985. O'Gara scored 48 points and was chosen to tour again with the Lions in 2005. Wilkinson and Stephen Jones were preferred, however, and he only made a brief appearance in the third Test of a series that New Zealand had already won comfortably.

He returned to Munster and helped them to the 2006 Heineken Cup against Biarritz. His form for club and country continued to improve and he was soon rated the best standoff in the northern hemisphere. Ireland failed to perform at the 2007 World Cup, however, and there was constant media attention regarding his private life.

He distanced himself from the press and kicked Munster to victory over Toulouse in the 2008 Heineken Cup. Ireland then negotiated a tough autumn international series that included wins over Argentina and Canada. He became the record points scorer in Six Nations history as Ireland cruised to their first Grand Slam in 61 years in 2009, although it needed a last-minute drop goal to seal the win against Wales at the Millennium Stadium.

He embarked on his third Lions tour in 2009 but only made the bench for the first Test in Durban, which resulted in a narrow loss for the visitors. He came on late in the second Test in Pretoria but it was his illegal tackle on Fourie du Preez that gave Morne Steyn a shot at goal when the scores were level at 25-25. Steyn kicked an incredible penalty from 50 metres to condemn the Lions to a series defeat and James Hook took O'Gara's place for the third Test, which the Lions won comfort-

ably to restore some pride.

O'Gara won his 100th international cap against the Springboks in 2010 but he was now facing competition for his place from Jonathan Sexton. Both men went to the 2011 Rugby World Cup and Sexton started the first three games. O'Gara returned for the crucial match with Italy and he retained the jersey for the quarter-final defeat to Wales.

Thereafter, Sexton became the first-choice standoff, and by 2013 O'Gara was only on the fringes of the squad. He retired at the end of the season as Ireland's leading points scorer and second in the all-time list for caps behind Brian O'Driscoll. A legend in his own lifetime for the drop goal that sealed the 2009 Grand Slam, O'Gara now coaches Racing Metro in France.

A legend in his own lifetime for the drop goal that sealed the 2009 Grand Slam, he finished playing for Munster in 2013 as their all-time leading scorer with 2,625 points, and since then has held coaching positions at Racing 92, Crusaders and La Rochelle, where he is their new head coach.

Name: Ronan John Ross O'Gara
Born: 7th March 1977, San Diego, USA
Position: Fly-half
Height: 6'0" (1.83m)
Weight: 183lbs (83kg)
International career: 2000 - 2013
International caps: 130
International points: 1,083
Honours: Six Nations Triple Crown (2004, 2006, 2007), Six Nations Grand Slam (2009)

O'Kelly

Malcolm O'Kelly was born in Essex but he returned to Ireland and went to secondary school in Dublin. Having left Trinity College with a degree in engineering, he joined Leinster for a year but then came to London with the Irish exiles. Having been capped at youth and Under-21 level, he made his senior debut for Ireland against New Zealand in 1997.

Over the next 11 years O'Kelly grew into one of the modern game's true legends. An unsung hero in the engine room, he provided the Irish pack with immense power, a safe pair of hands in the lineout and tireless work in the loose. He was selected for the 1999 World Cup but Ireland suffered a shock defeat to Argentina in a quarter-final playoff. The side

Over the next 11 years O'Kelly grew into one of the modern game's true legends. An unsung hero in the engine room, he provided the Irish pack with immense power, a safe pair of hands in the lineout and tireless work in the loose.

had been in the doldrums for most of the decade but Warren Gatland finally sparked a revival at the turn of the millennium and come the 2000 Six Nations Ireland were a force once more.

England may have denied them a Grand Slam in Dublin in 2003 but Ireland qualified from their group at the World Cup later in the year only to run into a rampant French side that put them to the sword. France again proved their nemesis in the 2004 Six Nations but England were now a side in transition and O'Kelly drove the side to a Triple Crown.

In the 2005 Six Nations match against Scotland, O'Kelly broke Mike Gibson's record of 69 Ireland caps. Ireland secured another Triple Crown in 2006 and O'Kelly made his third World Cup in 2007. He was also a Lions stalwart on the 2001 and 2005 tours to Australia and New Zealand respectively, although he picked up an injury before the ill-fated Test series against the All Blacks and was withdrawn from the squad. He made his final appearance for Ireland during the glorious Grand Slam of 2009 but played on with Leinster for another year.

Name: Malcolm O'Kelly
Born: 19th July 1974, Chelmsford, England
Position: Lock
Height: 6'8" (2.03m)
Weight: 261lbs (119kg)
International career: 1997 - 2008
International caps: 92
International points: 40
Honours: Six Nations Triple Crown (2004, 2006, 2007), Six Nations Grand Slam (2009)

LEFT Malcolm O'Kelly secures lineout ball

O'Mahony

A master of the dark arts and a natural leader, Peter O'Mahoney has captained Ireland U18, Ireland U20, Munster, Ireland and the British and Irish Lions. He plays primarily as a flanker but can also play at number 8.

He made his first start for the full national side against Scotland in March 2012 having won the IRUPA Young Player of the Year award for the season.

RIGHT Natural leader Peter O'Mahony

O'Mahoney played in all five games of the 2013 Six Nations and four of Ireland's games, picking up a Man-of-the-Match award against Wales, in their championship winning 2014 Six Nations. He started every game the following as Ireland retained their title – the first time Ireland had won back-to-back championships since 1948-49.

He played in the early rounds of the 2015 Rugby World Cup before aknee injury in a pool game against France ruled him out of the remainder of the tournament.

He continued to play regularly and well for Ireland and was made Man-of-the-Match in Ireland's 13-9 against England in March

2017 – a victory that denied England consecutive Grand Slams and endeared him the hearts of the supporters.

O'Mahoney started every game for Ireland as they won the 2018 Grand Slam and at the end of the deciding game against England, he gave his winner's medal to an Irish supporter with Down's Syndrome.

In the absence of the injured Rory Best, he captained Ireland to an historic series victory against Australia in June 2018 – Ireland's first since 1979 - with Mahoney winning his 50th cap in the third test.

Before that, O'Mahony had had a mixed debut for The British Lions in which he actually captained the Lions in their first test defeat against New Zealand (the 11th Irishman to ever captain a Lion's test team) but was controversially dropped from the squad all together for the second and third tests along with his former team-mate Brian O'Driscoll.

Commented the Independent's Alan Quinlan: " You've got to feel for Peter O'Mahony because he didn't do much wrong to be dropped but no-one can ever take away the fact that he captained the Lions in a Test. An incredible achievement that shouldn't be glossed over."

Name: Peter O'Mahony
Born: 17th September 1989 Cork, Ireland
Position: Flanker, Number 8
Hieght: 6'3" (1.91m)
Weight: 236lbs (107kg)
International career: 2012-present
International Caps: 68
International points: 10
Honours: Six Nations Grand Slam (2018), Six Nations Championship (2014, 2015, 2018)

O'Mahoney started every game for Ireland as they won the 2018 Grand Slam and at the end of the deciding game against England, he gave his winner's medal to an Irish supporter with Down's Syndrome.

O'Reilly

As a teenager, it only took Tony O'Reilly five senior appearances to play his way into the Ireland team. Four matches later, he was called up for the 1955 Lions tour to South Africa. He promptly broke the tourists' try-scoring record but, as a wing with lightning acceleration and a devastating sidestep, Tony O'Reilly always seemed to be in a hurry. If the tour made his reputation, his 15 tries in 16 games – including two in the Test series – cemented his legend.

Although Barry John was treated like pop royalty in 1971, O'Reilly was the sport's first superstar. On the 1959 trip to New Zealand he destroyed his own scoring record, which, given the different circumstances of today's tours, is unlikely to be beaten. He ran in 22 tries in 24 matches, including four in the Tests, one in each international against Australia and two more against the All Blacks.

O'Reilly loved the freedom he found with the Lions that he didn't have with Ireland. With the world's best players inside him, he saw much more of the ball and he loved to come onto the gain line at full speed 10 or 15 times in a game. The Lions played beautiful running rugby and O'Reilly was perhaps the finest exponent of that style in the game's history.

When he retired in 1970, his Five Nations career had lasted for more than 15 years, a record only equalled by compatriot Mike Gibson. O'Reilly had been out of the side for six years but he was recalled in favour of would-be debutante Frank O'Driscoll, thereby denying Brian's father what would have been his only Test cap.

He promptly broke the tourists' try-scoring record but, as a wing with lightning acceleration and a devastating sidestep...

Name: Sir Anthony Joseph Francis O'Reilly
Born: 7th May 1936, Dublin
Position: Wing
Height: 6'2" (1.88m)
Weight: 206lbs (94kg)
International career: 1955 - 1970
International caps: 39
International points: 30
Honours: Lions Series Winner (1959)

...Tony O'Reilly always seemed to be in a hurry. If the tour made his reputation, his 15 tries in 16 games – including two in the Test series – cemented his legend.

ABOVE Tony O'Reilly fends off D J Davison of the Junior All Blacks whilst representing the Lions in 1959

Sexton

When Jonathan Sexton dropped a late goal to win the 2002 Leinster Senior Cup for St Mary's College in Dublin, it provided the first hint of the greatness that was to come. Within four years he was playing for the province, and by 2009 he'd announced himself to a wider audience with a breathtaking cameo against Munster in the 2009 Heineken Cup semi-final at Croke Park. He then took over from the injured Felipe Contepomi in the final and kicked 11 points, which included an outrageous drop goal as Leinster beat Leicester 19-16. He graduated to the Ireland A squad for the Churchill Cup and his 15 points saw off the England Saxons in the final.

Sexton collected his first Test cap in a thumping 46-10 win over Fiji during the 2009 autumn internationals. Ronan O'Gara had made the fly-half position his own over the previous decade but Sexton was no respecter of reputation or past achievements and he was deter-mined to make the berth his own. Injury ruled him out of much of the 2010 Six Nations, however, although he toured New Zealand and Australia in the sum-mer and shared the fly-half jersey with O'Gara for the subsequent Six Nations.

Sexton endured a mixed campaign by his high standards but he was retained for the crucial match against a Grand Slam-chasing England at Lansdowne Road. He slotted five kicks from six attempts and gave Declan Kidney's side a much-needed boost by steering them to a 24-8 victory in a World Cup year.

Sexton and O'Gara again shared fly-half duties at the tournament but, despite a rare and thrilling victory over Australia, Ireland came up short against Wales and were eliminated in the quar-ter-finals. Sexton returned to Leinster for the Heineken Cup and put in two huge performances as the province overcame

Montpellier and Bath. He also inspired Leinster to a second-half comeback against Northampton later in the year with two tries and 28 points overall that gave them an unlikely 33-22 victory.

Sexton barely featured in the 2011 World Cup but reclaimed his place for a disappointing 2012 Six Nations campaign that yielded only two victories over Italy and Scotland. Injury ended his next Six Nations early but he then signed a deal to join Racing Metro in France for the 2013-14 season. Ireland endured a torrid 2013 Six Nations and could only beat Wales but Sexton was still chosen to tour Australia with the Lions later in the summer. He scored a try in the deciding rubber of an enthralling series that the tourists edged 2-1.

Ireland won the subsequent Six Nations and racked up three consecutive victories in early 2015. Sexton was man of the match in the crunch encounter with England in Dublin but the wheels came off the Grand Slam after a narrow loss to Wales in week four. Sexton then guided Ireland to a big win over Scotland and helped secure the 2015 championship on points difference. The last five years have been the story of a superstar. As captain of Ireland, he started all five games in Ireland's Grand Slam in 2018, the third in their history; despite suffering a broken wrist and ruptured ankle he played the majority of the third test in the Lions' drawn series against New Zealand; and he was awarded the World Rugby Player of the Year in 2018 – the second Irish player to win the award after inaugural winner Keith Wood in 2001.

Name: Jonathan Sexton
Born: 11th July 1985, Dublin, Ireland
Position: Fly-half
Height: 6'2" (1.88m)
Weight: 203lbs (92kg)
International career: 2009 - present
International caps: 97
International points: 819
Honours: Six Nations Grand Slam (2018), Six Nations Championship (2014, 2015, 2018) Lions Series Winner (2013)

BELOW Jonny Sexton clears Leinster's lines

Slattery

With Roger Uttley and Mervyn Davies, Fergus Slattery was the final piece in a back-row jigsaw that is still considered the best in the game. They dominated the breakdown and blitzed the Springbok defence to help the British & Irish Lions claim their famous series win over South Africa in 1974.

Slattery made his name three years earlier, however, when in New Zealand with the 1971 Lions. As a 22-year-old, the Blackrock College flanker had only just made his Ireland debut but he played his way into the team for the third Test. Sadly he was then sidelined on the morning of the game with a fever.

Despite suffering concussion and losing two teeth in the infamous Battle of Canterbury, Slattery played in 12 of the 24 matches and earned favourable comparisons with Irish legend Bill McKay who had been the standout player on the 1950 tour.

He dominated games from open-side

He dominated games from open-side flanker with his physical and abrasive style, his punishing pace and his eye for a gap. At the breakdown he was peerless, recycling ball that he had no right to win.

flanker with his physical and abrasive style, his punishing pace and his eye for a gap. At the breakdown he was peerless, recycling ball that he had no right to win, and ensuring that the Lions could mount more attacks than they would have otherwise. Indeed he should have been awarded a try in the final Test of the 1974 tour that would have given the visitors a 4-0 series whitewash. The scores were level at 13-13 when Slattery touched down but the referee hadn't seen him ground the ball and in the days before video evidence he couldn't award the try. He then blew for fulltime before the Lions could attack from the five-yard scrum.

Slattery was named captain for Ireland's tour of Australia in 1979. The hosts were expected to trounce the men in green but in Ollie Campbell the Irish had the finest standoff of his generation. Campbell kicked the visitors to victory in Brisbane by 27 points to 12, and he added all nine points in the second Test to give Ireland a 2-0 series win.

Slattery finally retired from international rugby after 14 years with 61 Ireland caps and another four for the Lions.

Name: John Fergus Slattery
Born: 12th February 1949, Dún Laoghaire, Ireland
Position: Flanker
Height: 6'1" (1.85m)
Weight: 205lbs (93kg)
International career: 1970 - 1984
International caps: 65
International points: 12
Honours: Lions Series Winner (1971, 1974), Five Nations Championship (1973), Five Nations Championship and Triple Crown (1982)

LEFT Fergus Slattery slips a tackle on the 1971 Lions tour to New Zealand

Stockdale

Jacob Stockdale has only been in the Ireland team since 2017 but he was on fire during their Grand Slam year so he arguably deserves to make the book for this alone.

He scored seven tries in the games against Italy, Wales, Scotland and England – setting a new record for the most tries in a single Six Nations championship – and was also voted as the Player of the Championship.

As if this wasn't enough, in November 2018 Stockdale scored the try that secured Ireland their first ever victory against the All Blacks on Irish soil.

Stockdale needed only eight test appearances to run in 10 test tries, the fewest by any Northern Hemisphere tier 1 player in the professional era.

He began his rugby journey at Ballynahinch RFC Minis and upon leaving school in 2014 played his

He scored seven tries in the games against Italy, Wales, Scotland and England – setting a new record for the most tries in a single Six Nations championship – and was also voted as the Player of the Championship.

club rugby with Queen's University. He represented Ireland at two U20 world championships making a significant impact at both tournaments including the run to the 2016 Final.

His forceful running and eye for the try line caught the eye of Ulster and after an impressive first provincial season he was called up to the Ireland squad for the summer tour of USA and Japan where he made a try-scoring debut.

Stockdale's form fell off during the Rugby World Cup in 2019, culminating in a particularly off-colour performance against the All Blacks in the quarter-final, but still in his early twenties his game-breaking ball-carrying and try-scoring are still massively potent forces.

Not not one to rest on his laurels either, he is working on improving his defence: "It's something that was seen as a bit of a weakness before but I've worked really hard on that in the last couple of seasons – and I'm not finished yet. My high-ball work in the air is coming along, too, and is something I want to turn into a strength, to dominate in the air and go after balls. If you can catch cross-kicks, it can be a 30-40m gain for the team."

Name: Jacob Stockdale
Borm: 3rd April 1996
Lurgan, Northern Ireland
Position: Centre, wing, fullback
Hieght: 6' 2" (1.89m)
Weight: 220lbs; (100kg)
International career: 2017-present
International caps: 28
International points: 80
Honours: Six Nations Grand Slam (2018)

LEFT Jacob Stockdale charges down the wing

Stringer

Peter Stringer initially struggled to be taken seriously as a rugby player on account of his small size but he was a scrum-half of real talent who joined Munster in 1998. The first of his 230 appearances for the side came against Ulster, and he played his first Heineken Cup match against Perpignan the following week. Munster made it to the final of the tournament in 2000 but they lost to Northampton by a point. Two years later, Neil Back deliberately knocked the ball out of his hands at a crucial scrum and Leicester went on to win. He finally won some domestic silverware when Munster won the 2002-03 Celtic League but by then he was already an established international.

He made his debut against Scotland in the 2000 Six Nations and he became an instant hit, appearing in 76 of Ireland's next 85 matches. Ireland had struggled to adapt to professional rugby in the late 1990s but Warren Gatland's side was now built around Brian O'Driscoll in the centre, a half-back axis of Stringer and Ronan O'Gara, and a powerful but mobile pack of forwards.

Ireland had a shot at a Grand Slam in 2003 but England overpowered and outplayed them in the decider in Dublin. Although they then lost heavily to France at the World Cup, Stringer played in all five matches and was so consistent with his distribution, as well as earning a reputation for bringing down big men with huge hits, that Ireland dominated the 2004 Six Nations. Their Grand Slam aspirations were dashed by another defeat to France, however.

Stringer was overlooked by Sir Clive Woodward for the 2005 Lions in New Zealand but his form with Ireland saw him make crucial contributions on the way to a second Triple Crown in 2006. A third followed in 2007, although Ireland were disappointing at the subsequent World Cup and Stringer only played in two of the pool matches.

The men in green finally realised their potential in 2009. They'd been trailing Scotland by three points at halftime but Stringer made a crucial break before supplying Jamie Heaslip with the killer pass. Ireland won the match 22-15 and only had to beat Wales to secure the Grand Slam. Ireland almost blew their opportunity, however, and they were behind with two minutes to play. Stringer kept his head a delivered another crucial pass for O'Gara to drop the winning goal.

He wasn't selected for the 2011 World Cup in New Zealand and he retired from international rugby immediately. He carried on playing club rugby for Bath, Sale and Worcester before retiring from professional rugby in 2018 in his early 40s.

Name: Peter Alexander Stringer
Born: 13th December 1977, Cork, Ireland
Position: Scrum-half
Height: 5'7" (1.70m)
Weight: 161lbs (73kg)
International career: 2000 - 2011
International caps: 98
International points: 30
Honours: Six Nations Triple Crown (2004, 2006, 2007), Six Nations Grand Slam (2009)

BELOW Stringer watches O'Gara have a shot at goal in Ireland's match against Scotland at Murrayfield in 2007

Trimble

Andrew Trimble went to Coleraine Academy and played with distinction in the Ulster Schools Cup. He developed into a fearsome runner who was equally comfortable on the wing or at centre, and he made his provincial debut with Ulster at the age of 19.

Having starred against Cardiff at the Arms Park in the Celtic League, he was selected for the national team for their autumn series clash against Australia at Lansdowne Road despite only having eight Ulster caps under his belt. He made something of an impression, albeit in a losing cause (14-30), but he retained his place and scored two tries in a 43-12 win over Romania the following week.

Trimble made the squad for the 2006 Six Nations and scored his third Test try against France. Ireland went on to complete a memorable Triple Crown and he was chosen to remain with the squad for the 2007 Rugby World Cup. It was a disappointing tournament, however, and Ireland also struggled in the 2008 Six Nations, winning only two matches. Groin surgery ruled him out of the side's summer tour and he hadn't rediscovered his form in time to join the Grand Slam-winning side of 2009. He then needed another operation to remove a bone splinter from behind his knee.

He rejoined the side for the 2009 autumn internationals and played so well as a replacement against Fiji that he was back in the starting line-up for the opening clash of the 2010 Six Nations against Italy. He only made one more appearance in the narrow win over England at Twickenham before returning to the left wing for a one-off Test against the All Blacks in New Plymouth. Trimble then missed the two-point defeat to the Springboks in Dublin but he was recalled for the 20-10 win over Samoa and the 29-9 victory against Argentina.

Having missed the biggest game of the autumn against New Zealand, he was deemed fresh enough and hungry enough to be included in the 2011

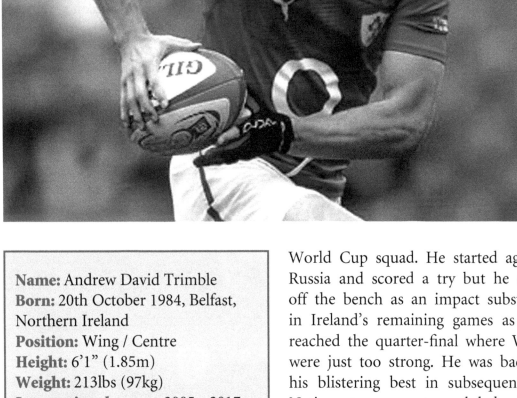

Name: Andrew David Trimble
Born: 20th October 1984, Belfast, Northern Ireland
Position: Wing / Centre
Height: 6'1" (1.85m)
Weight: 213lbs (97kg)
International career: 2005 - 2017
International caps: 70
International points: 85
Honours: Six Nations Triple Crown (2006, 2007), Six Nations Championship (2014)

World Cup squad. He started against Russia and scored a try but he came off the bench as an impact substitute in Ireland's remaining games as they reached the quarter-final where Wales were just too strong. He was back to his blistering best in subsequent Six Nations tournaments and helped the national team clinch the title in 2014 with Trimble scoring in a final nerve-jangling victory against France – to give Brian O'Driscoll the perfect send-off in his final test for the country.

Wallace

David Wallace moved to Cork and was educated at Crescent College. He developed into a fine rugby player and joined Munster at the age of 21. He made his debut against Connacht in 1997 and also played in that season's Heineken Cup against Harlequins. He had a fabulous 2000 and scored the only try of the Heineken Cup final but Northampton kicked three penalties and won by a point.

More solid domestic displays saw him return for the Triple Crown in 2006 and as perhaps the best open-side in the world he guided Munster to the European Cup.

His explosive power and pace at the back of the scrum saw him selected for the national team for their autumn series match against Argentina later the same year. Another solid showing at the subsequent Six Nations meant he toured Australia with the British & Irish Lions in 2001, although he was overlooked for a Test berth.

He suffered a series of injures over the coming seasons and only made sporadic appearances for Ireland in the next five years. More solid domestic displays saw him return for the Triple Crown in 2006 and as perhaps the best open-side in the world he guided Munster to the European Cup. The 2007 World Cup was a massive disappointment, however, but he bounced back to help Munster to a second European crown in 2008.

He was instrumental in Ireland's glorious Six Nations Grand Slam in 2009. Such was his stature within northern hemisphere rugby that he earned a place with the Lions on the subsequent tour of South Africa. He secured a Test berth instead of Martyn Williams but the Springboks were just too strong in Durban. Wallace retained his place for the second Test in Pretoria but crucial errors at the death allowed the hosts to claim the series by the narrowest of margins. He then came on as a replacement in the final Test and helped the tourists to a well-deserved 28-9 consolation victory. Serious knee injuries ended his dream of World Cup glory when he came off injured in the final warm-up match before the 2011 tournament in New Zealand.

Name: David Peter Wallace
Born: 8th July 1976, Limerick, Ireland
Position: Flanker
Height: 6'2" (1.88m)
Weight: 231lbs (105kg)
International career: 2000 - 2011
International caps: 75
International points: 60
Honours: Six Nations Triple Crown (2004, 2006, 2007), Six Nations Grand Slam (2009)

LEFT David Wallace stays focused during a break in play

Wood

Keith Wood began his career with Garryowen, helping them to all-Ireland titles in 1992 and 1994 before joining Harlequins. He proved himself a versatile, mobile, powerful, try-scoring hooker and, having already cemented his place in the national team, earned selection for the 1997 Lions on their tour of South Africa.

His contribution to the score that won the series for the tourists summed up his unorthodox style. His throw-in to the lineout was unexceptional but it was his break down the blindside and kick to the Springbok corner that had the hosts scrambling to defend a position from which they conceded territory. The Lions duly secured possession and Jeremy Guscott kicked the decisive drop-goal. It was this added dimension that gave the Lions the edge and he was on hand again during

the 2001 tour to Australia, a year in which he was voted the IRB Player of the Year.

His performances leading up to the tour saw him vie for the captaincy with Martin Johnson but, despite losing out to the Englishman, he remained a central influence on the team's fortunes and morale. He skippered the side against Western Australia in Perth and was the key man in the front row during the Test series. Never lacking in confidence, he even went for an outrageous 50-yard drop goal in the first match.

His form for Ireland was always consistent and he was selected for the 1995 World Cup in South Africa. The Irish were thumped by a Lomu-inspired New Zealand in their first match but they recovered to beat Japan easily and then edged past Wales to reach the quarter-final. France were too strong, however, and the Irish were soundly beaten 36-12. Four years later, Wood scored four tries in Ireland's remarkable opening victory over the United States, and they qualified for the knockout phase after a 30-point win over Romania. However, in one of the upsets of the tournament, the Irish were then beaten by Argentina. Wood's last World Cup in Australia was hugely disappointing: they may have beaten Romania and Namibia convincingly, and then avenged the defeat to Argentina, but a narrow loss to Australia preceded a humiliating 22-point defeat to France.

Wood retired from international rugby after the tournament but his record as a player is impressive: 58 Ireland caps and 15 tries (a world record for a hooker), with five caps for the Lions on two tours. He now works for the BBC and The Daily Telegraph as an informed and articulate commentator on the game. In 2014 he was inducted into the International Rugby Board's Hall of Fame.

Name: Keith Gerard Mallinson Wood
Born: 27th January 1972, Killaloe, Ireland
Position: Hooker
Height: 6'0" (1.83m)
Weight: 234lbs (106kg)
International career: 1994 - 2003
International caps: 63
International points: 75
Honours: World Cup Quarter-final (1999, 2003), IRB Player of the Year (2001)

LEFT A young Keith Wood during the presentation of his Sportsman Shield

Design & Artwork: ALEX YOUNG

Published by: G2 RIGHTS LTD

Written by: LIAM McCANN AND JULES GAMMOND

Foreword by: OLLIE CAMPBELL

Lightning Source UK Ltd.
Milton Keynes UK
UKHW052354181120
373654UK00006B/32